# ZAMBELLI

## THE FIRST FAMILY OF FIREWORKS

## By the Same Author

*Rehobeth, and Its Quiet Resorts*, Arcadia Publishing, 2003

*22 Friar Street*, Flower Valley Press, 2002

*Jacob's Trouble*, Renaissance Alliance Publishers, 2002

*Heartbroken Love* (pen name: Gianni Bonanno), Renaissance Alliance Publishers 2002

*Wallops Island, The Government's Love Affair*, Arcadia Publishing, 2001

*Chincoteague, A Barrier Island*, Arcadia Publishing, 2000

*Thy Brother's Reaper*, Renaissance Alliance Publishers, 2000

*Images of America, Ocean City, Volume I*, Arcadia Publishing, 1999

*Images of America, Ocean City, Volume II*, Arcadia Publishing, 1999

*Troublesome Grammar*, Garlic Press, 1999

*Grammar and Sentence Diagramming*, Garlic Press, 1996

*The Last of the Wallendas*, New Horizon, 1993

*Move It!*, Dembner/Barricade Books, 1989

# ZAMBELLI

## THE FIRST FAMILY OF FIREWORKS

### A STORY OF GLOBAL SUCCESS

GIANNI DeVINCENT HAYES, PH.D.

PAUL S. ERIKSSON, *Publisher*
FOREST DALE, VERMONT

**Library of Congress Cataloging-in-Publication Data**

DeVincent Hayes, Gianni

Zambelli : the first family of fireworks / by Gianni DeVincent Hayes.

p.   cm.

Includes bibliographical references and index.

ISBN 0-8397-9299-9 (pbk.)

1. Fireworks—United States. 2. Zambelli Internationale. 3. Zambelli family. I. Title.

TP 300.D48 2003

662'.1'0922—dc21

[B]

98-022327

---

ISBN 0-8397-9300-6 (hardcover)

Design by Eugenie S. Delaney

Thank you to the following people for their wonderful photographs:

Angel Art Ltd. Photography, Bob George Photography, Britt Pierson Photography, Clarkson & Associates, LLC, Chip Clark Photography, Corbis-Bettmann, Hagley Museum Library, Jeff Behm Photography, Joe Marcus Photography, Kevin Horan/Chicago, Middleton Evans Photographer, E.J. Morris Studio, Streamline Video, Inc., Mount Rushmore and South Dakota Tourism, Rick Dinoian Photography, Susan Wethli, Ted Thai Photographer, George R. Zambelli Jr., M.D.

A special thanks to all who supplied photos of their spectacular displays.

Fireworks illustrations by Mark Spielvogel

Cover photograph by Angel Art Ltd.

*With eternal love and gratitude, I dedicate*
*this book, and all the hard work, time, and energy*
*that went into creating it, to my family and loved ones*
*and to all the Zambelli family members.*

# Special Thanks

Because of their assistance and help throughout my writing of this book,
I extend my personal gratitude to the following:

Marcy Zambelli, who has been my right-hand person; without her help and input, I couldn't have accomplished this. She has put much effort into this project, and has been a godsend to me.

George Zambelli, Sr., for his wealth of knowledge about the business, and his willingness to help when needed.

Connie Zambelli for her endless support, reassurance, and composure.

George Zambelli, Jr., for his advice and information; to his wife and children, for their generous cooperation; and to his office staff, for their help when needed.

Donnalou Zambelli and her daughters, who have been understanding and prompt in responding to my requests.

Annlyn Zambelli for passing on the materials I needed, and for serving untiringly as a liaison.

Danabeth Zambelli for assisting in the acquisition of materials, and for her positive attitude throughout the project.

Ivy Fischer Stone, my agent at Fifi Oscard Literary and Talent Agency, New York City, for her direction and support.

Paul and Peggy Eriksson, *Publishers*, for their understanding, patience, and excellent work.

My mother, and my brother and his family, for their encouragement.

My husband, Jim, and daughters Marta and Brynne, for easing my home and family responsibilities, for making no demands on me while researching and writing, and for their immeasurable encouragement and praise.

Last but not least, the Zambelli workers at headquarters, in branch offices, at the plants, and all over the world, for their time, input, and assistance.

**Special Note:** On behalf of the Zambelli family and the author, a heartfelt thanks to the late Sue Twyford for her friendship, kindness, and assistance in the preparation of this book.

The Zambelli family also would like to thank the good Lord for all the blessings given to them.

# Contents

*Color illustrations follow pages 24, 64, and 100*

# Preface

When I was young, I was as fascinated by fireworks as I was afraid of them. I can remember, when I was a mere child, how my father would take my brother and me outside on the Fourth of July and light snakes and sparklers for us. While my brother frolicked with the sparklers, making them streak through the air, wind in circles, or twirl like batons, I'd stand silently watching the snakes fizz and curl into nothingness. What caused them to do that prodded me into liking the art of pyrotechnics.

Then when I heard about cherry bombs—and how dangerous they were—I grew even more interested in pyrotechnics, as well as alarmed at their explosive power. Support of this consternation came in the form of two accidents—to a relative, the other to a dear friend—that occurred years apart.

So though I had met head-on with the power of explosives, I also had grown to love their beauty, as seen in fireworks shows that throb and pulsate with natural power, lighting the sky in an array of rainbow colors and patterns while sounding off barrages that vibrate one's heart. I learned, too, there was none better at displaying this splendor and energy than Zambelli Fireworks Internationale.

The Zambellis can do anything—from developing the basic nighttime and daylight shows to executing elaborate computerized and electronic firings featuring brilliant and breathtaking theatrical presentations. They have shot fireworks off barges; from ground level; off the tallest buildings; indoors, outdoors; on stages; choreographed and synchronized to music, with dancing water and other acts, via special effects.

They're the leaders in creating original and unequaled extravaganzas, and they've done shows for kings and queens, U.S. presidents (having also recreated the "Great Seal"), Super Bowls, world's fairs, national conventions, and such galas as the Statue of Liberty anniversary celebration, papal visits, and White House concerts. They've exhibited in nearly every country on the planet. Their cache of fireworks ranges from hummers, salutes, strobes, and weeping willows to parachutes, shells, stars, and gerbs. And they're always ahead of their competition. They produce nearly 2,000 fireworks shows on America's Independence Day alone, and about twice as many as that, annually, all over the globe—by far the most presentations of any existing fireworks company on this earth.

It is their love of fireworks (and food: the recipes in this book are "Zambelli originals") that has pushed me to seek out the world's most famous fireworkers and write about them. Zambelli Internationale, Inc.—"the First Family of Fireworks"—shows how a little ingenuity and a lot of regard for each other and what they do can make a difference. This is a family who has traveled nearly every inch of the globe; a family who gives much of their time, expertise, and profits to charities and the needy; a family who upholds the old adage that "blood is thicker than water," and whose members dedicate their lives to each other.

— *Gianni (Nan) DeVincent Hayes, Ph.D.*

# Prologue

S leet pelts the hillsides of New Castle, a town under 30,000, nestled in the cold, arctic-like tundra of Pennsylvania's Lawrence County, about forty miles northwest of metro Pittsburgh. Founded in 1798 by John C. Stewart, it's fashioned after New Castle, Delaware, and laid out similarly to Philadelphia. By the 1840s, the town boasted canals, a bolt and nut factory, and a glassworks.

Growth escalated to the point where New Castle—one of the fastest-growing areas nationally—turned into a "city" by 1869. With the arrival of the steel industry in 1890, it became known as "the Tin Plate Capital of the World." A surge of European immigrants swelled the city's population from 11,600 to 28,339. Then, in 1913, a destructive flood suffused New Castle, affecting the employment base and slowing its steel production—a problem that grew worse through the years. So the city weathered many a travail, including a loss of population and the aging of its infrastructure. Thus, New Castle—like many old Northeastern cities—had to diversify once the decline in steel production blanketed the nation.

Yet, in spite of its ills, the downtown core still shifts and sways in a rhythm of its own. Though unemployment remains high, with a few jobs available in food, plastic and metal manufacturing, retail, and agriculture, the city pushes on. Promenading with a plethora of recreational activities, the area is known for its Amish farmlands, state parks, factory outlets, restaurants, historical sites, outdoor attractions, cultural activities, art galleries, playhouses, and dance companies.

Rolling hills offer a picture-perfect landscape for any painter. And when snow dusts the knolls and mounds, a sense of

*President Kennedy on White House balcony overlooking the South Lawn, watching a Zambelli fireworks display in honor of the king of Afghanistan.*

nostalgia whisks through one's insides, making one yearn for those times framed in Norman Rockwell paintings. New Castle fulfills this longing.

Along one area of its heath-covered cliffs, bare trees tower, and iced yews conceal nearly 1,000 acres of guarded land and buildings. It is under security because volatile powders permeate the grounds, as this is where Zambelli manufactures and stores its fireworks. While the city struggled with unemployment at the turn of the century, Antonio Zambelli struggled with moving his pyrotechnics dream from Italy to America. He chose New Castle because its climate was similar to Caserta's weather, not realizing that his dream would turn into the world's largest manufacturer and exhibitor of fireworks.

*New York City Fireworks Commissioner, George Plimpton, with George "Boom Boom" Zambelli during a fireworks extravaganza.*

Soon, other fireworks companies followed, making New Castle the "Fireworks Capital of America," with more than 25 percent of the nation's pyrotechnics business located here. Most of the fireworks companies folded . . . except Antonio's.

Zambelli Fireworks Internationale has been written up in hundreds of major publications, such as *The Living White House*, Time-Life Books, a Smithsonian video, *Encyclopedia of Entrepreneurs* (Hallett, Anthony, and Diane; Wiley Publishing), and Sotheby's "The Estate of Jacqueline Kennedy Onassis," among others. Sotheby offers about one display:

> [Zambelli] fireworks began . . . The original outburst was so monumental that the President's Secret Service agent and the King's bodyguard leapt forward to protect them . . . the most spectacular display ever . . . White House switchboard was inundated with telephone calls . . . Kennedy was enchanted and . . . the press wrote rave reviews about the fireworks . . . .

In the July 1998 issue of *Wall Street*'s "Smart Money," fireworks expert George Plimpton referred to Zambelli Internationale as "one of the oldest fireworks families in the country," adding that Pittsburgh's Independence Day fireworks show was most memorable because it was fired from five barges on the three rivers, with two three-minute-long grand finales or encores.

The July 13, 1998, issue of *Time* magazine featured an article on George Sr. and his son. It noted that "Zambelli is in an elite group of 'the country's foremost players' . . . [having done] the Statue of Liberty celebration in 1986. It did four presidential inaugurations, the Desert Storm troop return, the pope in Toronto, and, perhaps most important, the Elvis Presley stamp unveiling. . . ." George Sr. says

*A Zambelli fireworks fanfare in celebration of the 100th birthday of the Statue of Liberty on July 4, 1986.*

tions—with several of them underscoring their incredible pyrotechnics show above the four presidential faces on Mount Rushmore in honor of the $56 million restoration of the four busts—they recently have appeared on the History Channel and the Learning Channel in national documentaries. Zambelli Internationale Fireworks will continue to be featured on national shows, such as Travel Channel programs, among many others.

Zambelli expends a lot of time, energy, and money in acquiring and maintaining a respected reputation. George Zambelli, Sr., the son of Antonio Zambelli, has done just that.

This book looks at how George has managed to build a small fireworks business into one of the world's largest and most successful enterprises. It looks at how he maintains that image while splitting his time with family. This is a unique individual; this is a unique family. Thus, this accounting offers a special insight into both. Vibrant color photos allow readers to peer into the faces of these people, as well as get a glance at the buildings behind locked gates and the offices where creative juices flow. And not least of all, this book permits a look upward at the skies, which may explode at any second with a Zambelli display.

You'll walk away with a sense of what America is all about: a family with immigrant roots who live the American dream of working hard, treating others with respect, and giving all they can—the best of themselves, their product, their philosophies.

*A salute!*

the company did well over 15 million in business last year."

In addition to appearing twice on the Discovery Channel, as well as in many publica-

# ONE

# Connie and George Zambelli, Sr.

## "MOM & POP" BUSINESS OWNERS

Z AMBELLI INTERNATIONALE, though a family-owned, "mom and pop" operation, is anything but the neighborhood soda shop. Instead, it's a solidly built monolith run by George Sr. himself, with the assistance of his devoted wife and loyal children and a faithful staff who are more like family than employees. But thanks to the "pop" part of the operation, the one-time puny company has been built into a megabusiness that does about 3,500 fireworks shows a year, with nearly half occurring on the Fourth of July alone.

But this business took decades for George to fashion into the establishment it is today. This he did while working other jobs; yet he always knew he wanted to head the world's largest fireworks company, so he set out to reach that goal. In the process, he has created a legacy for his

*Connie and George Zambelli still enjoying fireworks together*
*after more than a half-century of marriage.*

*Corporate headquarters of Zambelli Fireworks Internationale, Inc., in New Castle, Pennsylvania. There are regional offices all over the world, including Florida and California. The company is more than a century old.*

The walls of the long corridor leading to the boss's office boast framed, signed pictures of George with luminaries such as every U.S. president from Kennedy on, David Letterman, several prime ministers, Pope John Paul II, various CEOs, the Marine Corps commandant, magazine and newspaper editors, radio and television VIPs, singers, and actors; and remembrances of Zambelli displays for jubilees such as the canonization of Mother Seton, the premiere of the movies *Angels in the Outfield*, *Pocahontas*, and *Hercules*; as well as for the Orange Bowl, endless coronations, war victories, rallies, galas, and scads of other glittering celebrations.

At the end of the long hall, tucked in a corner, sits the head honcho of fireworks, real estate, restaurants, and hotels, surrounded by numerous impressive wall hangings of famous people and memorial events. A spacious and bright office with lustrous wood, it houses a large desk and all the trappings of a corporate president, but the room seems too neat and orderly to belong to George, who comes across

children, who have worked in the business with him since each was a child, so like father, like children. And though George Sr. knows his four daughters and one son are awed by his business acumen, he rests easy in also knowing that at any point they can step into his shoes and, with the help of his industrious staff, continue the corporate machinery without missing a beat.

A first glimpse of this "corporate machinery" can be seen in the four-story office. The large Zambelli office complex reflects shiny mahogany and polished walnut and cherry desks. The entire floor is offset with offices filled with files: in cabinets, on floors, smothering desks, covering chairs, concealing windowsills and bookshelves; files that hold the specs of the 3,500 shows George does yearly. This doesn't count what's stored on computer, for every office has its own advanced high-tech system.

*Michael Eisner, Disney chairman and CEO, with George Sr., relishing the Zambelli fireworks show for the premier of* **Angels in the Outfield.**

*At the White House, Nancy Reagan thanks George for his outstanding fireworks presentation for the Congressional Picnic in 1990.*

as, and even looks a little like, a preoccupied and disorderly Einstein. Those who know Zambelli appreciate his creative genius. Yet, as distracted and absentminded as he seems, he can instantly put his finger on a particular file buried among hundreds of others and remember events, dates, and times as though he were reading from a script. When he barks orders, everyone moves quickly, and no one second-guesses this man, who is the quintessential expert on fireworks. If anything, he serves as the authority for all others, including his competitors. His ability to wow, woo, and will anyone he meets is extraordinary. His dedicated office staff, though

exhausted from trying to keep up with him, maintain a devout loyalty to him and his company and are always ready to go that extra distance for him.

At the opposite end of George's office—way down the other side of the corridor—sits the clients' waiting room. It looks much like the other cluttered rooms—more framed articles hang here, and more files lie on the couch, on chairs, and in corners. The waiting room is one of George's favorite places, and one that he has taken over in much the same way he has conquered every other space in the building. It is in the clients' waiting room that he relaxes a moment and reflects on his hectic day. Sitting with

*George Sr.'s parents, Maria Gueseppe and Antonio Zambelli, from Caserta, Italy.*

his legs crossed, one arm resting over the back of his chair, his tie loosened for the first time since early morning, and a manila file balanced on his lap, corporate CEO, general manager, and president George Zambelli reminisces.

## Antonio Zambelli's Dream

Says George, "My father, Antonio, mastered the artistry of fireworks in Caserta, Italy, around the late 1800s, and brought his pyrotechnics talents to America in 1893." He adds that when his father saw "The Lady," he took off his hat in deference to her and held it to his heart. When he got off the boat and touched foot to Ellis Island, he stopped and kissed our American soil: "My father traveled the wicked seas, endured the crowded boat, and sweated through diseases, just to start a new life in the Land

of the Free to give his children every chance. He wanted a strong pyrotechnics company, but the language barrier prevented this. I saw the potential for it and decided, when young, to pursue it."

This wasn't something George had talked over with his father at length, because George isn't a vocal man. And when he did exchange ideas with his father, it was in Italian. George claims, "Of all my siblings, I spoke Italian the best." His siblings included Joe and Annabelle, the oldest—both deceased. His sister Congetta is still fiery at 90. Carmen—now deceased—was next in line, then George, followed by the twins, Louis and Rita (deceased). The seven children got along well and were obedient to their parents. In fact, George says, "I never argued back with my parents; we were expected to defer to them and show respect. The lack of respect by today's young people is part of what's wrong in society." And like his father, George expects that same kind of respect from his grown children, along with a corollary regard for women, especially.

*Antonio's family, circa late 1920s. Standing left to right: Annabelle, Joseph, Congetta, Papa Antonio, Mama Maria. In front, George, Louis, Carmen, and Rita. Louis and Rita are twins.*

"America," he adds, "needs more discipline, and we individuals in this country need to be more accountable and responsible for our actions instead of trying to blame others and find excuses and scapegoats for what we did wrong or didn't do right. Whatever happened to 'character' and good ol' morals?" George hopes he and his wife, Connie, have passed the same values on to their children. With a smile on his face, he adds, "I think we did. I'm proud of every one of them."

George admits his father was strict and that in many ways he, himself, was just as strict with his children. But while growing up, George enlisted "my mothers influence to get around my dad. I was Mama's pet, and if I wanted something and my father said no, I got my mother to convince him." George explains that his father was old-fashioned, with basic traditional ideas: "He regularly said prayers and the rosary in Italian." With that wry smile on his face, he adds, "I was a good boy."

His sister Congetta agrees: "He *was* a good boy—not like the rest of the brothers. He was my mother's favorite, and she gave him everything he wanted." This elderly woman, with the brightest eyes and smoothest skin for a person of her age, smiles the same kind of grin her kid brother, George, does. Born in Italy, where she lived with her family until they moved when she was eight, she offers insight into her life in America: "My mother tended the chicken coops and her garden, which she loved, and my father directed everybody and everything and got results by yelling a lot; Italian was spoken in our house. It was expected that we all would help with chores, and be there for one another. I can remember washing clothes on a washboard, cooking early Sunday dinner, and doing whatever our father wanted."

"My dad was more bark than bite," concedes

*George graduating with a bachelor's degree in accounting and insurance in 1946 from Duquesne University in Pittsburgh.*

George. "It just took a little manipulating to get him to see possibilities other than his."

And what kinds of "possibilities" might those be?

"Convincing him I wanted to try my hand at the business. He wouldn't let me play with fireworks when I was young, so how was I going to persuade him to let me do it for a living?" Yet, at seven, George had already rolled firecracker tubes, and at 16 he became a shooter.

His father told him he had to go to college first, so unlike his siblings, George attended Duquesne University—an urban Catholic institution run by the Holy Ghost Fathers that sits atop a bluff in downtown Pittsburgh. There, he majored in business, intending to build his father's fireworks dream into a conglomerate. He had big ideas and big plans—all of which he singlehandedly made come true. He attributes much of his success to returning home after college graduation in 1946 with a degree in accounting and insurance. "I had the indulgences of my family to be successful," he says.

## Boom-Boom Zambelli

The pyrotechnics industry continued to grow on George. Knowing how much he wanted to make the family business into something respectable, he went to his brothers and sisters and proposed, "Let me take Pop's business concept and work with it, applying my college education and business background to create a fireworks enterprise we all can benefit from." Having the education, creativity, and a model to follow—his uncle Elrich Scarazzo, who succeeded wildly in the automobile business—George outlined a plan for the fireworks

*The lobby of Zambelli Fireworks in the Hotel New Penn (now called the Z Penn Centre) before renovations.*

company that proved equitable to all. "Elrich's wife, Bambina, was my mother's sister, and the two shared a lot with me. My uncle taught me the subtle things about salesmanship that go a long way in building solid customer relationships."

Congetta says, "Immediately we all agreed, because we knew what a hard worker George was, and we all respected him."

George strategized and began implementing his ideas. The fireworks company was time-consuming, and this coupled with running a hotel was akin to the Mad Hatter's skirmishes. Shrugging, George says, "I ran the fireworks business full-time, even typing my own letters, while also operating the Hotel New Penn (later called the Z Penn Centre), thinking my own family and relatives would take care of the dining room. And many did pitch in occasionally."

"Occasionally?" echoes his family, astonished. His wife, children, and relatives remember well how much time they devoted to cooking and serving in the restaurant, saying George's memory is a bit "weak" these many years later.

Congetta's daughter, Lucille Jute, tells a story that defines George well: "Everyone *had* to do time in the family restaurant, and Uncle George was no cupcake to work for. One night he made me go into work because he was short of help. He didn't care that I already had made plans, so I went in and waitressed. But all night he got on me about not working hard enough. He kept it up until finally, as I stood listening to him, I deliberately dropped the platter of butter, turned on my heel, and

walked out of the restaurant. I could hear him mumble in the background, 'What's wrong with her?'" Laughing, Lucille adds, "No matter how wrong or tough Uncle George was, my mother always sided with him. And why should I have expected anything else when she was the one who waited on him hand and foot, even did his laundry, when they were growing up?"

Lucille pauses, then interjects, "Sometimes Uncle George was so preoccupied with business that he was naive about life. This one time, I went to Aunt Connie's [George's wife's] house to get my hair dyed, since I knew my mom wouldn't let me. When Uncle George saw my hair he ordered, 'Fix it. Now.' I said to him, 'I can't just change it back at the snap of your fingers.'"

The practice of family members helping in the restaurant business remains today, as even the grandchildren throw themselves into cooking and serving. They, too, have stories to tell about their grandfather's drive and high expectations, though "Papa" has mellowed a bit over the decades. "Still, the narrowing of his brows, the grunt from his diaphragm, can say more than words themselves," offers one grandchild.

Just as George drove his family crazy, he showed as much drive in running his fireworks company. Having taken over the business, he worked both the hotel and the fireworks company from his cubbyhole in the hotel. He remembers the hours he spent on the phone calling friends and networking with others, as well as writing letters, making a point of getting to know key people in the community, and later expanding that to the entire country, and then to the world.

*Constance Jane Thomas before marrying George Zambelli, Sr.; she worked for Bell Telephone.*

"But I had the help of my family," George reveals, "especially my wife, who first caught my attention while I was still in college."

## And Then Came Connie

George beams when he talks about his wife: "While waitering in the hotel dining room, I'd see this gorgeous woman walking down the street on her way to work at Bell Telephone. I asked my aunt—the wife of the successful uncle in the car business—who she was, and she told me the woman was Connie Thomas. I was determined to meet,

date, and marry her. She was classy back then and is even more so now."

George's aunt introduced him to Connie, warning, "Don't interfere. She already has a boyfriend."

But George didn't care. He wanted to meet Connie and get to know her. "Besides," he says, "I wasn't afraid of competition. Look who won in the end." He flashes a cocky grin.

Although Connie had seen George through the restaurant's windows, she didn't formally meet him until later.

"And then she didn't like me," says George, shaking his head, as if such an impossible thing could happen. "But her parents and sister did, so I had them as allies." Not one to give up easily, as witnessed by his perseverance in pursuit of success, George persisted in imposing himself on Connie, and the more he did, the more she came around to liking him and then loving him. They were married in George's last year of college, in St. Mary's Church in New Castle, while Connie was still at Bell Telephone. But having just left school, and with debts to pay, he took his bride and set up house with his parents. There, his business whims were coddled, and he was given the space and support he needed to succeed. "For this, I'll always be grateful," says George. "Marrying my wife is one of the greatest blessings I've ever had. She's been a gift to me for the last 57 years."

Perhaps his other gift is knowing how to build a small business into a giant enterprise. He owes part of his success to postwar bliss when "the economy was in high speed, promotional companies made greater use of fireworks, and America felt a need to celebrate." Because of George's business

*George and Connie united in marriage in New Castle, Pennsylvania, in 1946.*

acumen and the many contacts he made working the phone and attending conventions, coupled with his honesty and finesse, he was able to clinch deals.

"From there," begins George, "I advanced the company through high-technology, music, computers, and choreography, along with a number of other innovative projects and programs. To make a company the biggest and the best, you have to be resourceful and inventive, willing to take risks and meet challenges. I not only put in a great deal of money, as well as my self, but I also did a lot of charity events to build a good reputation and to help others."

To determine how fine a fireworks display he was putting on for customers, as well as to learn about his competition, George made a point of seeing all of his own shows as well as many of his rivals'. Even today, he attends at least a hundred performances yearly and a number of his competitors' as well.

Smiling, George says, "Over the years, my lovely wife has been at my side at almost every one of those shows I've gone to."

## Connie Thomas

"Well," begins Constance Thomas Zambelli, as she sits on a stool at the kitchen counter in her resplendent two-story home, where her impeccable taste is reflected in the drapery, wallpaper, mirrored walls and ceilings, elegant dining room, and gingerbread carpentry, "I did accompany George to most shows, but not as many now, because I have less energy than he." She smiles. "I remember how I'd pack up the kids and wing them off to some city or country because George had a business deal. For the children and me, it was a vacation, but for him, it was work. Yet he always managed to find time for us."

Slim, petite Connie is a paradox—quiet and restrained, soft-spoken and demure, and yet compelling and forceful when need be. The second she walks into a room, this small dynamo grabs everyone's attention. A certain aura about her punctuates the air, and you sense you're in the presence of someone special. It's in the way she carries herself, how her eyes sparkle, the velvety tone of her voice. She electrifies a room and makes heads turn in her direction. Her very person emanates elegance and panache. And still, she manages to endear herself to others instead of putting them off, despite her

*George's family, circa 1966. Back row, left to right: Donnalou, Connie holding Danabeth, George Jr. Front row, left to right: Annlyn, Marcy, George Sr.*

grandeur. She once owned and operated Lauder School of Charm, and had taken modeling courses in Florida; she also had studied art and interior design at Youngstown College (now Youngstown University). Her soft, short laughter doesn't match her quick, broad wit. She has an astute sense of the absurd and gets a kick out of the incongruous or the ridiculous. By anyone's standards she remains the beauty she was in her youth, and it is understandable how her daughters turned out to be equally enchanting.

The mother of five—George Jr., Donnalou, Marcy, Annlyn, and Danabeth—Connie herself was a product of a large family. Four children were born in America to Italian parents from Caserta, Italy—the same town where George's family originated. She doesn't know if or when her surname was ever changed, but she does know that her family structure was much like her husband's, who, she admits, "was not my intended when I first met him. I had planned on marrying another. His family and my family knew each other even though George and I hadn't officially met."

She recalls how on the morning of VJ day she had been standing on the sidewalk in downtown New Castle with friends, joining in the victory celebration. Out of nowhere, a debonair, princely looking young man approached her and introduced himself. In no time, he had engrossed her with his conversation as well as with his charm, polish, and magnetism. When he said to Connie, "Allow me to drive you and your friends through the streets in celebration," Connie, bewitched, eagerly agreed: "It was the best time I ever had. The entire scene—with the ticker tape, excitement, and this nice-looking man—was something out of a storybook. Like Houdini, George had magically captivated me." It was July 1945 when they met and took their first ride together; by January 1946, they were engaged. On June 20th of that same year, they were married and have been riding together ever since.

Connie says, "He never told me he was into fireworks until about halfway through our engagement. If I had known earlier that he had such an 'explosive' nature," she laughs, "I might have reconsidered." On reflection, she adds, "Right from the beginning, I appreciated his drive and ambition. I knew he wanted to make something of his family's fireworks business, and I had no doubt he would succeed." Living with George's family helped her understand her new husband and his family life, and she knew George liked children and wanted a team of his own. "Thank goodness, we had our parents to help babysit," she laughs, thinking of how the children arrived one after another arrived.

On February 6, 1948, the first child arrived: George Jr. Speaking like a true mother, Connie boasts, "My son was a bright, perfect child, and he had a nice group of friends. He obeyed his father and me, did errands, and showed a lot of ambition, just like his dad. He had a paper route in town, near the hotel, but he ate all his profits or bought matchbox cars with them. He liked both: eating and cars." She remembers her son saying he wanted to grow up to be a doctor, "but I'd say, 'Oh sure,' and of course he did just that. He really was a good boy." When pressed, Connie admits, "Okay, he was a little rambunctious. If a firecracker went off, everyone pointed a finger at George Jr., because he loved fireworks."

> "Right from the beginning, I appreciated his drive and ambition. I knew he wanted to make something of his family's fireworks business, and I had no doubt he would succeed."

When young, George Jr., made the transition from helping out in the hotel to toiling in the fireworks business. Connie says she didn't worry too much about her only male child working at the plant, simply because "I trusted my husband's judgment, and I knew he'd never put our son in danger."

The golden-haired boy was soon challenged by the addition of another child—his sister Donnalou, who arrived on August 7, 1950. "I think that date's correct," mulls Connie. "All my kids' ages seem to run together."

Connie describes her first daughter as a go-getter, a perennial honor student, always a leader, and forever striving for perfection: "She got that from her father. She was Snowball Queen . . . and all those dance recitals her father and I attended. From an early age, Donnalou thought about going into pharmacy, but then decided on becoming a dentist. She fulfilled that dream. I remember those days my mother and I would drive from New Castle to Beaver Falls to visit Donnalou at Geneva College, but before college and during the summers she put in time at the hotel, waitressing and bookkeeping. *Everyone* in the family worked in the hotel in one capacity or another, and then for the fireworks company, too. Even today, Donnalou will consult for the business, go to displays to check out our rivals or the quality of our shows, and entertain clients—all this between managing a family and her dental practice. She did her share of work in the hotel/restaurant business, too. We all were recruited more than we volunteered." Connie's eyes flash with her wide grin as she shifts her position on the stool. "My breaks came with the birth of my children," she laughs.

The third baby to arrive was Marcy—the middle child: "She was a ball of energy from the day she was born. I called her my 'party girl.'" Connie beams at the thought of how her ebony-haired beauty with the big eyes came squealing into the world on October 12, 1955. "Her rich black hair was just like her father's. She had lots of friends and really enjoyed people, even as a child. Later, she taught at the Barbizon School."

Marcy was such a good baby that she made Connie want to have more children, so 15 months later Annlyn arrived, on February 28, 1957. "She was a vivacious and animated child," Connie describes, "so much so that the family would ask each other, 'What office is Annlyn running for?' She bubbled over with enthusiasm for life, got involved in all kinds of activities, like cheerleading.

But as she got older, she grew more reflective and reserved. Now her entire existence is focused on her own family: daughter Constance, son Michael, and husband Michael. She works hard at corporate headquarters for her father, and although she takes her role of wife and mother seriously, if we didn't stop her, she'd run the sweeper 10 times a day. Always she's chaperoning the kids around, helping Constance with dance, or little Michael with sports. She's an excellent mother."

Annlyn's antithesis is little sister Danabeth, the baby of the family, born on September 6, 1963. She is lively and mirthful, and has a laugh that at once electrifies everyone around her and pulls them into her world of delight. She—and her sister Annlyn—cherished their roles of Princess of Apple Blossom. And though Danabeth can be as witty and wry as her mother, she also can be as serious and business-like as her father. Being the youngest, Danabeth

*George Sr. describes mortar box setups to White House chief ushers on the South Lawn.*

seems to view life from a cockeyed position that allows her to make merry.

This she did with her entrance into the world. Says Connie, "My obstetrician told me that Danabeth wouldn't be born before my husband returned from his visit to the White House, but since Danabeth was never one to follow rules, she arrived about the same time President Kennedy learned of the birth of his stillborn son. So George with George Jr. nearby, stood drinking champagne in the Yellow Room and had to leave the White House and rush home to see his new baby girl.

"Because Danabeth was the youngest, she accompanied my husband and me wherever we went on business, so she got to see the world at a young age. She was an old trouper, staying up late to watch fireworks with us, half asleep." Connie's expression reflects those fond memories: "If Danabeth's arrival into the world didn't topsy-turvy Washington, then her attendance at the University of Maryland College Park did. George and I spent a lot of time in D.C. with her since the campus is near the capital, and we wanted to make sure those values we instilled in her stayed with her in a city that was more than on the loose side."

Being the only child at home, Danabeth traveled the world with her parents and met high-level executives, celebrities, and royalty. Through time she proved herself to be an asset to her parents by hostessing clients and speaking knowledgeably on fireworks, acting much like her father's personal executive. She knew her parents' clients as well as her mom and dad did.

"Danabeth handled herself admirably on the business circuit," says Connie, "and was just as vivacious when not with business contacts. One time when the three of us were traveling and only George could get a seat on the plane, Danabeth and I vol-unteered to wait at the airport until we could board another flight. Poor George thought we were sitting around the airport, moping, when actually Danabeth and I had left the terminal and gone shopping at a mall. She was as fun and energized then as when we finally met up with our clients."

## George and Connie

Still seated in the kitchen, with her husband near, Connie goes on to speak about the amount of time she and George spent with their children, and now, how her children spend their time with their own offspring. "My grandchildren have good parents," she says with a hint of pride in her voice.

Spending a lot of time with the children seems to be a hallmark of all three Zambelli generations, from Antonio on. As busy as George was running the hotel and fireworks businesses, he still set aside time for his wife and children.

"He never missed the children's PTA meetings or school events, and he always came home to dine and spend time with them. At night, he'd take them out for a treat, and while on vacations, he'd entertain them at the beach. Always he put our children first," says Connie, "no matter how busy he was."

George shrugs: "It's nice of my family to think that, but I've always felt guilty for not having spent even more time with them."

His children describe him as stern. Connie looks at him and bats her eyes. "I don't think my husband was unnecessarily hard on our children; I just think he wanted them to do the right things. I, of course," she says with a smile, "was the defender of the children." She leans forward and whispers, "I could always get around George with a smile. If he hasn't caught on in 57 years, he never will."

George rolls his eyes.

As the company's vice president and "roving ambassador," Connie says, "I adapted early on to our active life. I've sat in on business meetings, taken part in transactions, and often substituted for George when he couldn't go somewhere. In fact, while I was in China with Danabeth, the Chinese asked me to name their new shell. I dubbed it 'Diamond in the Sky.'" She adds, "It was nothing for George to call me from work to say he was bringing home a client for dinner. He still does that. It seems like there's always someone visiting."

George nods. "Connie's been a godsend to me . . . the ideal wife and mother." He glances at her. "She's a real asset. It's like I always say: She's a class act."

"Oh George." She looks at him. "Yet, he's the one who just goes and goes."

A typical day places George at the office by around five or six in the morning, where he meets with Howard (Howie) Simmons, the plant manager. Together they go over business matters, review plant happenings, and discuss long- and short-term strategies. Howard updates George on every aspect, whether major or insignificant. Then George touches base with other key personnel in the company, sorts out what needs to be done during the day, follows up on loose ends, and gears up the arriving staff for a new day. At a decent hour, George gets on the phone and makes contacts. His lunches at his hotel restaurant are business meetings. "The art of selling," says George, "is getting customers to like you and to grasp that they're buying something distinctive."

George believes that success comes from keeping one's word and from going that extra mile for customers. "My kids think I'm nuts if I spend a whole day pulling strings for clients—say, tracking down Steelers or Pirates tickets—but to me, that's the secret of victory. It's that added effort that often makes a difference in acquiring a sale or clinching a deal. Business is run differently today. In my time it was those little things that counted a lot. Where, back then, a handshake and a smile sealed a deal, today it's reams of legal papers. Sometimes I wonder if I'm a dinosaur in a silicon valley."

Dinosaur or not, the one thing that hasn't changed through the decades is the secrecy of the fireworks "recipes"—those chemical formulas that are kept as sacred as holy water. The recipes for Zambelli Internationale are secured and held in secrecy in the vault. Says George, "They're protected. They've been handed down by my father and are written in Italian. There's never a reason good enough to share them."

The basic ingredients of all fireworks are public knowledge, but the specific combination of chemicals, the milling of the powder, and other factors that give each fireworks company its unique shells are not published, except in those black books kept in safes. So, then, how do competitors discover what makes one type of shell more special than another?

George cocks his head: "We buy the shell, disassemble it, and reproduce it in our own bunkers." He's quick to add, "Though fireworks companies might be rivals, most of us cooperate with each other." In fact, years back George heard about a competitor's intent to hold a surprise party for the family elder. In secret, George sent his men over to the family's place to set up and fire one of the most extravagant fireworks displays ever. George recalls the event fondly and becomes ever more delighted when he recounts how appreciative they were.

Zambelli's company is known not only for a voluminous number of annual displays but also for its fireworks manufacturing processes; it is one of

the few remaining pyrotechnics companies world-wide that manufactures its own shells. But that, too, is changing. Clarifies George, "The world has become so much more accessible that it's more economical to buy shells from other companies around the world than to go through the time, manpower, and expense to make our own. Years ago, it was the other way around. Because of this, I see us manufacturing less in the future. I'd rather focus more on the computer, electronic firings, and close-proximity production, and continue to be on the leading edge, than try to compete with foreign production."

George adds that if a company in another country is offering affordable shells that aren't quite up to his standard, he does one of three things: shows the company how to manufacture them to his specifications; sends his people to do the manufacturing; or ships the company's components home to improve them. "I'm obsessed with quality," admits George.

As far as the future of Zambelli Internationale goes, George says with a shrug, "We'll continue doing what we do best—whatever it takes to make a client happy."

Connie interjects, "The children and I would like him to slow down, and I want him to spend more time with me, now that we're getting older. Not only do we have great kids, but we also have wonderful grandchildren whom we could enjoy more. Our children have been trying to get him to take more vacations, but George always manages to turn them into business meetings. Right, George?" she asks in her soft voice.

"You've got to make hay while the sun shines," answers this workaholic spouse, who can still, at his age, wake at sunrise and go late into twilight. "I

wouldn't mind seeing the company expand," he admits, as though he hasn't heard a word of protest from his wife. "I'd like to have my children and their spouses more involved, as well as having everyone live and work here, at corporate headquarters. To get bigger than we are—and we're the largest right now—we'd need more high-tech equipment, more capital, more plants, more warehouses, and more staff."

Connie gives him a look, and he shifts in his chair before adding, "The greatest celebrations have just begun. With the new millennium—sitting right in our laps—everyone is celebrating everything, and loving it!"

"Don't forget," inserts Connie, "how much business has picked up for such events as New Year's Eve and First Nights."

George agrees: "Fireworks for New Year's has become big; we do more shows for it now than ever." And he should know, since he's the one usually called in to perform them.

Connie says that if her husband persists in the business, she'll persist in accompanying him whenever she can: "I'll go on the road with him just to keep him straight. He does try to accommodate me, satisfy me, when I'm with him." She cuts her husband a look and then adds, "As long as I can stop and eat, I'm happy."

George shakes his head, gives his famous quasi-smile, then remarks, "It's been a good business." He leans over and kisses his wife, his philosophy emblazoned in the minds of others: "I expect to pass through this life but once. Any good that I can do or any kindness that I can show to any fellow creature, let me do it now. Let me not defer it or neglect it, for I shall not pass this way again."

# TWO

# George Zambelli, Jr., M.D.

## SURGEON EXTRAORDINAIRE

T HE SOLIDLY BUILT, curly-haired gentleman likes to make people laugh, in spite of his seriousness about his medical practice and his love for his patients. The child in Dr. Zambelli pulsates with enough raw energy to burst a dam, wanting to get out and enjoy life. It's not unusual to find him standing before his nieces and nephews, tossing M&Ms into the air and catching them on his tongue like a gecko lizard trapping its prey. And the more you watch him, the more you enjoy him. His mother grins widely at her son's mischief, giving him a private nod that only a mother's son can decipher. He may be a renowned, hot-shot surgeon in his own right, but to his family he's not only brilliant, but also a lovable guy with a zest for life.

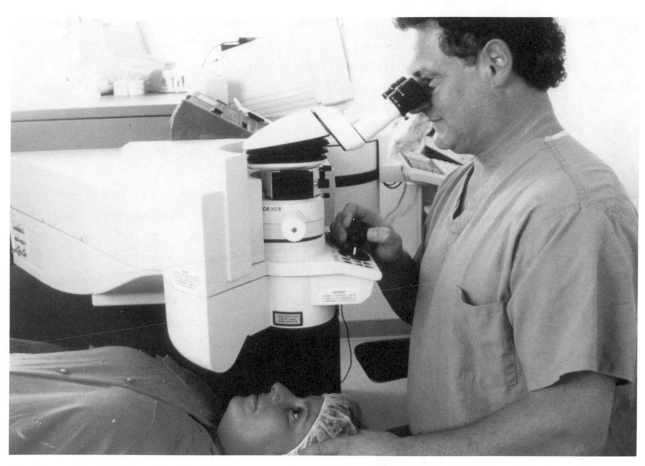

*Dr. George Zambelli, Jr. performing Lasik eye surgery on a family member in his Rochester, Pennsylvania, clinic.*

The firstborn and only son of George and Connie Zambelli, George Jr. makes clear his long-held interest in fireworks remains active and uncompromising. While operating on a cataract patient is painstaking work, operating a fireworks display at his father's business is wildly exhilarating. He does both with deftness and skill. While intensely analytical and precise in a surgical suite, he can be comparatively creative and loose at a fireworks location. In fact, even today he plays a major role in helping design pyrotechnics programs for the family business. Having worked side by side with his father since childhood, George could step into the business at any given time and direct the operation. But it is those growing-up years, when he first learned the business, that he credits for giving him his love of fireworks.

## Childhood

Dr. Zambelli says, "My life started out a year early. My dad did that—put me in school a year ahead. The principal at St. Vitus, Sr. Rosemary, argued with my father, said it wasn't healthy to do that to kids, but my dad stood firm—not yelling, just insisting—and finally he wore the nun down. So I remained the youngest in my class. But no one could stay angry with my father, because he was always doing nice things for others and performing charitable acts for the community, the church, and schools."

By his own admission, George Jr. behaved obediently in school, though he looked forward to going to his father's office to help out. His father would tell him to call a certain person for him, and the little boy would get on the phone and ask the operator to connect him with the party. "Back in those days, it was a human voice on the other end of the phone, so I could tell the operator who I wanted. When the operator would try the number but couldn't reach anyone, I would feel like a bigshot by saying, 'Could you please keep trying, and call back when you get our party?' Then when she'd call back, I'd run and get my father. This is how I first learned about the importance of one's work."

From the time George Jr. was little, his father instilled in him a solid work ethic. George Sr. believed what his parents had taught him—that in America one can achieve anything with honesty, integrity, and hard work. George Sr. embodied that for his children his whole life. Like many immigrant descendants, the senior Zambelli lived his parents' philosophy. George Jr. saw how his grandfather and father dutifully performed the same tasks over and

*George Sr. with son George Jr. reviewing a fireworks design for a July 4th celebration in Atlantic City, New Jersey.*

over again—rise early, eat, attend mass, go to work, return home to family, go to bed, and start all over the next day.

Thinking back to his childhood, George Jr. remembers affectionately how his grandfather, Antonio, who founded the fireworks business, would sit around the kitchen table with his son, George Sr. and talk about work. He put on fireworks shows until the day he died of heart problems. "But my grandfather was very 'old style,'" says George Jr. When the men sat, the women served the meal before joining their husbands at the table. Italian men were treated like kings, and the wives respected how hard they worked to provide for the family. The adults sat around the table, talking fluent Italian with each other, yet they never spoke to us children in their native language. I think they wanted us to assimilate American culture and not be hindered by the ways of the Old Country. Looking back now, I wish my parents had taught us Italian; being bilingual today has many benefits."

George Jr. smiles when he recalls how his grandmother always worked in her gardens. "It was tradition for our family and my aunts and uncles to visit my dad's parents after Sunday mass. I can still remember my grandmother hunched over in the chicken coop collecting eggs, or weeding in her vegetable patch, warning us kids, 'Stay-a outta my garden,' and then giving us a hug. That was the nice thing about growing up in a close-knit, ethnic family: You knew your parents and grandparents loved you in spite of how strict they were."

Like Antonio, George Jr.'s father was a stern disciplinarian; Junior explains, "My father had a way of looking at me that instantly told me when I had done or said something wrong. He was domineering but in a loving way. If, for example, I asked him for something and he said no, the answer was

no; there was nothing I could do to change his mind, and it was unlikely I would have tried anyway. He didn't want a lot of unnecessary chatter at the dinner table, and my sisters and I knew not to speak unless we were spoken to. My father was, and still is, a man of few words. He's never been the type to reveal his feelings; he only talks when he needs to. He assumed we kids knew what he was thinking. He has always had high expectations for each of us. But when he smiles, the whole world blazes.

"As the disciplinarian, my dad yelled when we misbehaved, while Mom was the peacemaker and protector. She never bucked my dad, but she had a way about her that could charm him into doing what she wanted. While my father went out and earned the dollar, my mom stayed home for us children. She liked it when we invited friends over; she'd cook an entire meal if we wanted it. She used to drive my sisters to school, though I had to walk, and she enjoyed doing things with us, going to the local park, shopping, or wherever we wanted to go. She dedicated herself to her family and the business. My dad, on the other hand, was the breadwinner who dedicated himself to work."

George Jr. recalls his father creating business deals even in social situations, such as at the Hotel New Penn. Tucked in the corner of an alley at Mercer Street, the brick hotel drew many customers from New Castle and the surrounding area, not only for its fine lodging but also for its fabulous food and hospitality. George Jr. remembers as a teen in the 1950s spending many an hour working

*From the time George Jr. was little, his father instilled in him a solid work ethic. George Sr. believed what his parents had taught him—that in America one can achieve anything with honesty, integrity, and hard work.*

at the business—from helping wait tables, operating the early-1900's water-powered elevator, and running the cable switchboard, to serving as a gofer for his father's fireworks company. With fondness, George Jr. recollects that "the elevator was one in which after closing the trellis-like gate with special gloves, I would pull the cable that ran from the top of the elevator through the floor. Doing this would start the cage moving its way up the cable. I would grab the cable and yank on it to stop it at the appropriate floor. I also played switchboard operator, so that when calls came in, I would plug the lines into the corresponding telephone extensions.

"Back then, my father was more known and respected for his hotel and restaurant connoiseurship than his fireworks because the latter was still growing. At the hotel restaurant, Dad would cook, serve lunch, and act as host. He had a little office set up in the back of the lobby where he ran both the hotel and fireworks business from the same rolltop desk. I used to do all the errands for him. He was always conducting business, sometimes very complicated deals. My father was work-driven, and so he negotiated deals wherever he went."

Because Senior was a busy and reticent man, and Junior wanted to learn all he could about the family business, George Jr. devised an information-gathering system that gave him insight into what his father was doing for a living. "I read all his letters. By studying my father's correspondence with other businessmen, I learned how both the hotel

*George Jr. before a fireworks production "lancing" a set piece (ground display) of First Lady Barbara Bush's dog, Millie.*

and fireworks companies were run. I think my dad privately gloated over my ingenuity." If his father needed a letter mailed, business supplies purchased, a proposal delivered, George Jr. jumped at the opportunity to help. "I was a gofer," he says, "but by doing that, I learned not only about the nature of the pyrotechnics business but also about people. It didn't take me long to decipher body language, so I soon mastered reading people's faces, their movements, voice tone. It's been very helpful to me later in life."

By age 12, Junior was toiling in his father's English Avenue plant, which "had different levels to it because of the hills. In one building, we made set pieces, like battle ships attacking each other, flags waving, presidential portraits. There, I learned to pound peg nails into wet bamboo or wood so that lances could be stuck onto nails. Sometimes I'd load the truck or dig trenches. Uncle Louie would show

me where to dig, and I'd do it with a posthole digger to set up the stationary pieces. Many times, I did all-around help in putting a show together. One summer I had plans to go to a Pirates baseball game, but my dad and uncle had other plans for me, so instead, I found myself working a show."

He laughs when he mulls over whether he got paid for his work. "Gee, I don't remember getting a lot of paychecks. I helped because I wanted to, and because Dad told me to." Yet, his father limited some of the work his young son did because of the danger in the business. "My dad wanted me to learn; still, I knew he was overseeing everything I did and making sure I wasn't placed in any hazardous position. He particularly was cautious of my hands." No wonder, seeing that Junior had aspirations to become a surgeon, a career his father had envisioned for him. Those aspirations had been planted almost from the beginning. There was never any question whether George Jr. would go to college. His parents had given him no choice; quite simply, he would become a college graduate whether he operated the fireworks business or operated on patients.

"Next door to my family's house, lived a medical doctor," says George. "My father had always admired him, telling me that what a physician did was a worthy contribution to society. He wanted me to contribute in such a way. So ever since I was a kid, I had planned on becoming a physician. I even play-acted being a doctor."

Years later, he would "playact" the role of a bearded lady in the Orange Bowl's halftime show where he sat in a rocking chair on a float. "My dad volunteered me when the real bearded lady didn't show up for the ceremony, and since we were doing the fireworks that night, Dad thought it would be good to help the organization sponsoring it. Hey, I even got a standing ovation."

TOP: *Customized set pieces are designed by artists and built in many shapes and sizes. The Zambelli set piece is illuminated with 4- to 5-inch lances; thin rolled, cylindrical papers containing pyrotechnics powder that burn around 60 seconds each.*

ABOVE: *The nation celebrates the return of Desert Storm troops with a Zambelli show in Washington, D.C., June 1991. Stars and shadows are among the new pattern shells introduced at this event.*

LEFT: *One of many Zambelli fanfares at the Washington Monument over the past 60 years.*

*Fireworks fill the sky at the White House Congressional Picnic, 1990.*

*LEFT: A spectacular for the Pittsburgh Pirates at the original Three Rivers Stadium.*

*ABOVE: George's grandchildren, 1999. Back row, left to right: George III, Jessica, Amberlee, Summer, Alison; front, left to right: Jared, Michael Jr., George holding Alandra, Connie, Aubriana, Constance.*

*BELOW: Rising Tails and Splitting Comets illuminate the Ohio River during Thunder Over Louisville, the kick-off celebration for the Kentucky Derby Festival.*

*Cascading embers of Weeping Willows over Indiana and Kentucky.*

ABOVE: *Scenes at Thunder Over Louisville change rapidly. The televised event is the largest annual fireworks show in America. 3,500 feet of bridge, 18 barges, ten computers and hundreds of people work to coordinate the state-of-the-art fireworks extravaganza at Thunder Over Louisville.*

OPPOSITE PAGE: *Three nights of fireworks at Fair St. Louis light up the waterfront and St. Louis Arch, Gateway to the West.*

*A Zambelli Fireworks spectacle in the skies above Flagler Drive, West Palm Beach, Florida.*

*The Baltimore waterfront celebration, July 4th.*

*Sprays of green light up the bridge waters at Thunder Over Louisville, Louisville, Kentucky.*

Whether bearded lady, fireworks expert, or surgeon extraordinaire, George Jr. took his roles seriously. From childhood on, he geared up to becoming a doctor. But this didn't prevent him from spending time in his dad's fireworks business. "One of my most cherished memories of growing up at Dad's side in the business was the year 1959. I was 11, and it was a bright, sunny day when he took me to an All-Star baseball game. Knowing he was a workaholic, I figured I'd be lucky to have his attention for all of fifteen minutes. But to my surprise, he concentrated entirely on me during the time we were together, from the second we left the house until the minute we got back home. We talked about a lot of things that day. It was just the two of us . . . and he didn't transact one iota of business. Gosh, that was wonderful. Once you got my dad out of the business element, he was like any other father."

## College Years

J ust as that special day at the baseball game lovingly lingers in George Jr.'s mind, so does another time when the Georges had to meet a customer in North Carolina. Father and son stayed for three days in a big, old hotel—which George Jr. believes was the Biltmore Hotel in Ashbury—with no technological equipment (phones, faxes, computers) to distract the senior Zambelli. "It was totally relaxing," remembers Junior. "Just Dad and I enjoying one another's company, talking business, and yet sharing. I learned how proud Dad was of me."

Part of that pride comes from George Jr.'s hard work at school. Having received his bachelor's degree from Case Western Reserve University in Cleveland, he went on to medical school at St. Louis University. There he tried sorting out what kind of medicine he wanted to specialize in. While

he studied hard, he kept tabs on the business back home. The same was true when he studied ophthalmology at Ohio State University. During his third year in medical school, he found his love— microsurgery performed through an operating microscope at Bethesda Hospital in St. Louis. An operation was about to take place, and an attending physician asked George if he'd like to observe this specialized procedure, as ophthalmology was the only discipline at the time to use a microscope to perform surgery. George agreed. "Instantly, I fell in love with intricate microsurgery. I walked out of that operating room and knew what I wanted to do. From then on, I took all the ophthalmology courses I could."

Luck remained true to George Jr. when he was considering where to set up his practice. He had met someone who encouraged him to look into a new medical center that was combining three hospitals to form a state-of-the-art medical facility for the growing suburbs surrounding the large Pittsburgh Metro core. "At the time, it was referred to as the Beaver County Medical Center, but now it's called The Medical Center, Beaver— a subsidiary of Valley Health Systems," says George. "It's only about 20 or so miles from my hometown of New Castle. Now here was a gift in disguise. I could practice in a new hospital and become a name and not a number, and be within 20 miles of the famous high-tech medical nucleus of Pittsburgh as well as within 20 miles of my hometown and family, which allowed me to remain an integral part of our fireworks business. I had to take it, and I did. While setting up my practice, I did what I could to remain active in fireworks. I bought the company's first computer in the 1970s, and I sent publicity letters to every chamber of commerce in the country to let them know about our pyrotechnics skills." Likewise, George Jr. initiated the founding of the California fireworks office, too.

The rest is history, as the saying goes. George Jr. established a top-rated medical/surgical eye practice that brought in patients from all over—patients who now boast about his unequaled skills, his concern for them, and his great sense of humor.

On June 1, 1973, George Jr. married a nurse, Melanie Lynn Weiter, from St. Louis. "We got married in the Old Cathedral in St. Louis," says George Jr. "It's the first cathedral west of the Mississippi and so popular that you have to pick your wedding date a year in advance."

George and Melanie have two daughters. Alison, 26, has finished her post-baccalaureate pre-medical studies and is currently pursuing a career in medicine. Jessica, 23, is enrolled in the Physician Assistant program at Gannon University in Erie, Pennsylvania.. While both daughters have inherited their father's interest in the medical field, Alison and Jessica still maintain an interest in the family fireworks business. They, like their brothers, enjoy accompanying their father and grandparents on business-related travel as well as individually representing the Zambelli corporation.

All the Zambelli grandchildren are steeped in the family business and have learned how to conduct themselves in a mature and gracious manner. Oldest son George III, 20, is a freshman in college. He spends his summers at the fireworks plant working with his mentor and great-uncle, Louis Zambelli. As his uncle's apprentice, George III is learning the artistry and craft of pyrotechnics, as well as what it is that makes Zambelli fireworks unique. At home, on his computer, young Geroge learns the Fire One software program that the business uses to create, choreograph, and exhibit fire-

*George Jr. reviews computerized firing with his sons Jared (left) and George III, both of whom are following in the footsteps of their grandfather and father's in the fireworks business.*

works displays. The youngest of George Jr.'s children, Jared, 15, is attending North Allegheny Junior High in the Pittsburgh area. Jared is also interested in fireworks choreography and computerization. He, too, practices with the Fire One program and is especially interested in Script Maker—the program used to sequence and synchronize pyrotechnics shows.

"They've just assumed they'd be a part of it, even if it means holding a career during the day and doing fireworks at night," says George Jr. Both my sons have spent many hours at the fireworks plant in the computer firing training program, and can install the firing program for any show, as well as perform a host of computerized functions, such as testing the main and peripheral modules, doing squib testing, and setting the show clock and synchronization modes. Their training in electronic fire displays will no doubt become, at some point in their lives, an integral part of our family tradition."

Alison and Jessica think the same way. Says

Alison, "Like my father [George Jr.], I want to pursue medicine, but the fireworks company will always be a part of my life. I enjoy traveling with my relatives, being part of decision-making processes, and meeting people. I like being with my grandparents, too. Papa [George Sr.] is very intelligent, so I have to be on my toes when I'm with him. He keeps my mind racing, and is always trying to teach me something." Alison has the same warm feelings about her grandmother, as well as for all her cousins. "We are a really close family," she says, echoing her father's words. Alison, who has entered a post-graduate premedical program with the intent to enroll in medical school, adds, "Watching my father run his busy practice and still keep actively involved in the family fireworks business tells me that I can do the same."

Her sister Jessica is a Physician Assistant major who wants to follow closely, but not exactly, in her father's footsteps. "I'd like to do what my father does—work with patients and yet keep my fingers on the pulse of the family business. I can see myself consulting on fireworks, traveling, and meeting with clients, just as my dad does with his father."

## Present

George Jr., and Melanie find themselves busily maintaining the sprawling French-country home they've built north of Pittsburgh. It boasts a unique design of angled and high-ceilinged-domed structures, with six bedrooms, a rambling master bedroom chamber, steam room, tanning room, computerized theater room, whole-house stereophonic setup, an exercise room with serious equipment, recreation quarters with an entertainment area, pool table, and a host of other "playthings," as well as a library, reading room, and two laundry suites employing Melanie's numbered clothes-coordination system that could surpass any dry-cleaning operation. The interior of the house emphasizes a bird theme where wall paintings of birds and cages and other accoutrements accent the theme. Built into the first floor is a large compass pointing to true north. Near it is the antique roll-top desk that George Sr. had owned when he first conducted hotel and fireworks business decades ago. Says George Jr., "I remember how that little desk sat alone in the hotel's small alcove, then moved inevitably to a room of its own, then on to a whole floor, and eventually became part of a space that overtook nearly the entire hotel building." The desk has been passed down to Junior where it reminds him of his father's hard labor in helping him get so far in life. Indeed, Zambelli's large home is one of those things his father indirectly helped with.

In George Jr.'s home during Yuletide, Melanie sets up and decorates thirteen different Christmas trees positioned throughout the house. Outside, the grounds boast exquisite tiered landscaping with a 27-foot-high cantilevered retaining wall that supports the large pool, a fish pond with waterfalls, doll houses, and a tennis court. Accompanying all this is a six-car garage and carriage house, a sophisticated intercom system, and an outdoor cabana connecting to the interior of the house and sitting perpendicular to an underground tunnel that runs the length of the home to the garage and carriage house. Inside the garage is a Porsche Carerra—one of the original Vipers—reflecting George Jr.'s lifelong love of cars. Behind the garage a spiral staircase starts from the pool area and leads to an elaborate series of wafered decks and balconies at the back of the house. Melanie designed and decorated their entire ravishing home.

Just as George Jr.'s estate takes up much of his time, so does his ophthalmic microsurgical practice, Western Pennsylvania Eye Physicians & Surgeons, Inc., located in a metropolitan suburb of Pittsburgh. Dr. Zambelli has had a staff as large as 25, and has progressed from single-stitch cataract microsurgery to his "Z-incision," no-stitch, clear cornea phacoemulsification technique. He has been performing phacoemulsifications since his residency in 1977, at which time he was one of only a small percentage of surgeons worldwide certified to perform this delicate technique. Phacoemulsification is a type of ultrasonic procedure that removes cataracts via a high-speed titanium tip that vibrates at 52,000 cycles per second. The instrument fragments the cataracts and removes them from the eye with gentle suction. The procedure is a quick, painless, efficient technique using no "shots in or around the eye," only topical drops. Dr. Zambelli's patients are able to perform their normal daily and recreational activities immediately following cataract surgery, such as bowling, golfing, or dancing.

George Jr. has been involved with refractive surgery since 1983. As Medical Director of the Zambelli Laser Eye Institute, he serves Pittsburgh and the tri-state area with state-of-the-art Laser Vision Correction procedures, including Lasik. The thirty-to-sixty-second Excimer laser procedure allows nearsighted (myopic), farsighted (hyperopic), and astigmatic patients to experience a new kind of freedom from glasses and contact lenses. Zambelli uses the soft, cool beam of the laser to reshape the surface of the cornea to allow light to focus on the retina in order to improve patients' natural vision. With the safety and predictability of the Excimer laser, Dr. Zambelli has performed Laser Vision Correction on members of his own family. He states that his happiest patients are by far his Laser Vision Correction patients, 99 percent of whom drive without their glasses or contact lenses. Through Laser Vision Correction, Dr. Zambelli provides his patients with improved natural vision for active lifestyles—skiing, golfing, tennis, biking, swimming—without the hassle of glasses or contacts. George Jr. is enjoying his commitment to Laser Vision Correction and his continual dedication to excellence in eye care.

*Through Laser Vision Correction, Dr. Zambelli provides his patients with improved natural vision for active lifestyles.*

Zambelli's high profile throughout the world has led to a trip to the Orient, where he taught 100 Chinese surgeons his ultrasonic phacoemulsification procedure and his single-stitch and no-stitch techniques. Accompanying him was his father, George Sr., who mostly kibitzed with Chinese fireworks manufacturers, except for the one day he surprised George Jr. by suiting up for the operating room to watch his son perform surgery. "I always wanted him to do that," says Dr. Zambelli, who smiled with warmth and love for the elder. After all, it's part of the work ethic that father and son share.

"I work extremely hard," explains the younger George, recounting the long hours he spends studying patient charts, operating, seeing patients, and keeping up with medical insurance policies. "But as hard as I work, it still doesn't best my father's toils. The man is a walking dynamo. Do you know he can talk on seven or eight different phone lines at once?"

The son sees the father still adhering to his work philosophy after some fifty years of pressing himself mercilessly onward and over the top. And the senior expects his son to help whenever he's needed. "My dad was so used to my being there for him that he thought nothing of calling me and asking for help on a minute's notice. Finally, I had to ask him to give me at least a 24-hour warming when he needed me. Of course, he got that little smile on his face and said, 'I don't remember you giving me a day's warning when you needed me while you were growing up.' But I'm always here for him."

It's easy to picture the young, curly-haired, raspy-voiced physician pacing in his father's conference room, talking aloud to himself or humming a musical strain, as he works out ideas in his head for a fireworks show. He's in constant motion. He swings his arms or jabs with his fingers to emphasize a point, and if he disagrees with his father, he tells him so, but in the same even-tempered way he would talk to a patient. While creating a proposal or designing a show, father and son privately share a smile, enjoying one another.

As the father sits calmly, writing notes on a yellow tablet, making and taking calls, he eyes his son's pacing. Periodically, he comments to the staff around him, or rises to get something. Everything is at George Sr.'s fingertips because of his ability to organize well and to keep both his files and himself active. The tempo the elder George maintains amazes his offspring, who admires his father's ability to do all that he does on a daily basis. "My dad works from morning to night. He does an extensive amount of networking to maintain and build the business, and he knows how to contact anyone. He works from an agenda and oversees the entire operation."

As one of the world's largest manufacturers and exhibitors of fireworks, Zambelli Internationale grew big, fast. George Jr. is awed by how quickly his father expanded the business. "He always wanted to do fireworks, so when he graduated from college with a degree in accounting, he went to his brothers and sisters and offered to take over the business and expand it, giving each of them a percentage of the profits and various opportunities. His siblings eagerly consented, and my father—who's a man of his word—made sure they were all taken care of. Three of Dad's brothers worked in the company in a hands-on capacity while my father managed the day-to-day headaches. A third brother—my Uncle Carmen—helped out at the hotel and office. I used

*George Jr. and his family live in Marshall Township, Pennsylvania, 45 minutes away, but they enjoy family get-togethers, at least twice a month. Left to right: George III, Jessica, George Jr., Connie, George Sr., Alison, Jared, Melanie.*

to love working with Uncle Joe, who ran the old plant and supervised the manufacture and production for the aerial displays, for the Washington Monument shows. It was just magnificent. We've done work for every president beginning with John F. Kennedy. The first vehicle I ever drove was the White House tractor."

Over time, the business began growing about 20% per year, so the Zambellis have had to rebuild its infrastructure continuously. Corporate headquarters has a staff of at least 25 in off-season, and the manufacturing plants have another 30 to 40, not counting the reps stationed around the country, or the branch offices in Florida and California. So from that single desk in a little alcove soared an empire, with one large plant becoming two, and a work force numbering in the thousands on the Fourth of July.

"With the help and support of my mother, my dad did it all after he took over the business from my grandfather; this is the reason Dad wasn't home a lot when I was growing up. To make up for his absence, he began taking me, and later, my sisters, with him on business. He still does that today. His philosophy is if he can't be home with his wife and kids, then his wife and kids will be with him. He wakes early in the morning and is at the office by five, meeting with his staff, going online to check over the company. From eight-to-five, he's on the phone or in meetings, clinching deals, or he's out on the road or in the air traveling the world. Then, until nine or eleven at night, he's making other necessary contacts. To substitute for

> *"Considering the thousands of shows we do a year, and the few accidents we've had in over a century, having the safest record worldwide is quite an accomplishment."*

my father, every family member could work in the business and still not accomplish all that he does. Though supplanting him would be a real challenge, my sisters and I could meet it, and are doing so every day, as we're each becoming more involved and instrumental in the development, administration, and decision-making processes of the business. Should either of our parents decide to step down, we five children are prepared to carry on in their stead at a second's notice. After all, we've been training for this since childhood. We're fortunate, too, that the corporate staff is not only loyal to us, but that they're also very proficient at what they do. Most have been with us so long that they can do their jobs with their eyes closed." Junior grins. "Still, my father's energy is mind-boggling."

Besides George Jr. being impressed with his father's ability to run a plant employing a lrge number of workers, he's equally taken by by his dad's physical energy, though of late Senior has been coping with some ailments that befall anyone in his late seventies. "Yet," says George Jr. "Dad can span the Nashua Plant's expansive acreage as if he were a man of 45, and still not get winded."

In addition to what Dr. Zambelli calls "micro-managing" daily activities, his father also plans for the company's future. The son believes his father would like to have his children and grandchildren come into the business, so that he could pass down the family company to them. Already, George Jr. and his sisters are actively on the job in some capacity, but the elder hopes that the grandchildren will also take an interest.

"I would like for my children to work in the business," says George Jr. "and some of the older kids have already expressed an interest. Others are too young to understand the role they could play. But I think Zambelli Fireworks will go on, remain a family-owned company. My worry is whether we descendants can measure up to what Dad has done, or convey his sense of artistry and love for the business. My dad has years of experience behind him in negotiations and networking. He's a real charmer simply because he truly cares about his work and his customers. I imagine that when my sisters and I fully take over, things will change. We'll have to be more businesslike, whereas my father is more informal and casual. As our business constantly grows and the industry continues to change—with more paperwork, more rules and regulations, more computerization—our company will have to be run like a corporation instead of a 'mom and pop' operation. But I don't think any of us can ever transcend what my father has done and continues to do."

George Jr. sees signs that his father is mellowing, becoming a bit more relaxed. "Not much, though," says the son, who still accompanies his father on weekend business trips. "Now and then, he'll pause to catch his breath. Once at a mall I saw him slow down enough to look in store windows, even grab a bite to eat in the food court. If only for an instant, he was putting things aside to take advantage of the moment. Perhaps he's coming to terms with his own mortality."

But no sooner does young George think his father's beginning to learn how to appreciate life—even if late in his 70's—than he'll do something totally opposite, such as when all the Zambellis (grandparents, parents, children) go on a family cruise. "It frustrates him that he's confined on the boat. He's okay for the first few days, but then he starts with the pacing, looking out the ships windows, and I can see he's getting antsy and wants to get off and do business. Once, he asked me how far it was to swim from the liner to shore." George Jr. laughs. "It takes the whole family to hold him down because if we didn't, we'd find him setting off fireworks from the ship's deck."

# Competition

**B**eing involved in the family business allows George Jr. to survey the competition. Without a doubt, Zambelli Internationale has the lion's share of the market, performing thousands of shows a year, while competitors seldom do more than 100 to 700, and many do even fewer than that. Says George Jr. "Most clients contact three fireworks companies for bids when they're planning an event; two of the companies contacted are usually from the client's local or tri-state area while Zambelli Internationale is almost always the third. The reason we get called in to bid against fireworks companies in the client's geographical area is because we're the best and the largest; we shoot all over the world. Most pyrotechnics firms display only in their region, while Zambelli Internationale exhibits globally. By nature and tradition, fireworks companies are a competitive bunch, but at Zambelli, we have immense respect for our competitors, with whom we often work. My father is first on the phone to extend assistance if there's an accident at another company's plant."

George Sr. is often first on the phone calling up business as well. Junior says that in addition to working with repeat customers from decades ago, Zambelli constantly gets new business—"off the

*The two Georges enjoying a private moment together in the lobby of corporate headquarters.*

might be. We keep immaculate records, not only for our own knowledge, but also for the government. At display sites each shell is accounted for and kept safe from the public. A quality-check person makes sure there's proper distance from where debris may fall to where audiences stand. Nothing is overlooked. Whatever it takes to keep the public safe and to perform the most outstanding show, we'll do it. Spectators can rest assured that their experience at one of our shows will be a safe and enjoyable one." Enjoy, they do. After watching a Zambelli fireworks show, observers are exhausted from applauding exuberantly, ooohing and aaahing in exclamation. Everyone remarks what a fantastic experience it was and how stunned they were with the magic of the show, its raging power and spirited colors.

"The colors of our fireworks," says George Jr. "are brilliant and lustrous. We've created and mastered new images, such as crackling star shells, splitting comets, and spiraling crossettes. Also distinctive are our multibreak shells. And we're tops in computerization, along with the amount of inventory we have on hand because we manufacture our own, though we shop the world for other kinds of shells. We just do astonishing performances."

As we wind up our interview with fireworks consultant and laser vision surgeon Dr. George Zambelli, he sits on a stool in his spacious kitchen while his wife sets out grapes, cheeses, and crackers a few hours before they are to leave to attend a Broadway show in Pittsburgh. He glances outside the patio doors, watching snow fall, mumbling, "Maybe the roads will get too slippery to drive."

His petite wife cuts him a look. "We're going, George. I've been waiting to see this play."

George grins his enchanting smile—a smirk much like that of his father. It's understandable then why the old saying goes, "Like father, like son."

street"—based solely on the company's reputation for flare, service, unique and colorful displays, and safety history. Internationally it is one of the fireworks companies with the best insurance rating because of its outstanding safety record. Says George Jr. "When you buy fireworks, you should buy a company's reputation. Considering the thousands of shows we do a year, and the few accidents we've had in over a century, having the safest record worldwide is quite an accomplishment. We're proud of that, and we do everything we can to maintain it." Zambelli Internationale does more than routine safety checks to maintain the highest level of safety at the plants. "Our company knows where every shell is on our thousand acres, where every fuse and mortar are placed—right down to where matches

# THREE

# Donnalou Zambelli, D.D.S.

## SAY "AH-AH-AH-AWESOME"

DENTIST DONNALOU may require others to open their mouths wide, but she herself isn't one to speak a lot. A woman of few words—something she inherited from her father—Dr. Zambelli is second oldest. She sits at a table in a private dining room at Pittsburgh's Sheraton Station Square, where her entire family is assembled for dinner hours before the scheduled wondrous and majestic fireworks show is to be displayed for Pittsburgh's world-renowned Three Rivers Regatta. She's watched thousands of shows since childhood, but each is more special than the last. Her memories of life with Dad and Mom, brother and sisters, are warm. What remains fresh in her mind is how her father insisted that she and her siblings study all the time.

She says with a smile, "As young children, we couldn't read yet, let alone study. Ever since we were toddlers, my father instilled in us the importance and the value of an education. When my dad got something in his head, he wouldn't let go."

## Life With Father

Donnalou believes she always wanted to be a dentist . . . or that her father always wanted her to be one. After all, brother George was destined to be a doctor, and since she was second in line, the profession of dentistry seemed equally wonderful.

"I can still picture my father sitting at the supper

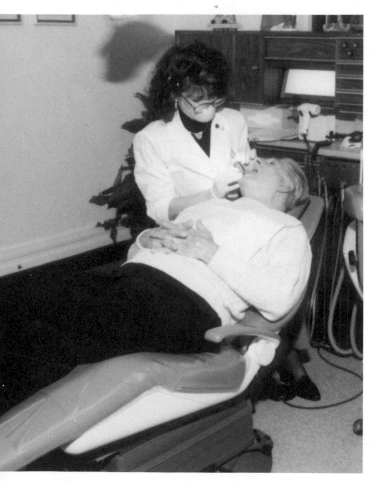

*Donnalou Zambelli, D.D.S., working on a patient in her office located a floor above her father's office.*

table, saying little except for how virtuous an education was. I thank him for teaching me that." Donnalou turns around in her chair and glances at her father, who's sitting at a large round table with his wife and others. "Dad was tough on us kids. He expected us to perform to certain standards, and he always wanted more out of us, believing that the more he demanded, the more he'd get. I think he was a lot like his parents. It was routine for us to attend Sunday mass and then go to my grandparents' house and have dinner, with hot, fresh bread. Dad's mother—my grandmother—was sweet, and she loved working in her garden. Dad's father, Grandfather Antonio, who started the fireworks business, always sat at the head of the table, not saying a lot, but directing others with his eyes, his facial expressions."

Quiet, stunningly pretty Donnalou has a way of forming a particular expression—a cross between a smile and the rolling of her eyes—that makes others laugh with her. "My father was something to deal with. He was very strict and headstrong—a real disciplinarian." She tells how he got involved in the hotel business and set up that small desk in a tiny hotel alcove: "It was this little room—a closet, really—where he conducted hotel and fireworks matters. I can still see him running around the hotel, taking care of the guest desk, cooking in the kitchen, serving meals, and selling fireworks in between." She laughs, likening her father's hustling about to that of a scurrying chipmunk.

Because of all the different jobs her father performed, he expected "everyone to help out at the hotel. If you could breathe, you were expected to toil right along with him. When I was young, I filled ice cube trays. Then I graduated to waitressing by the time I was in seventh grade. Always my father had events booked at the hotel, so instead of going out

and having fun with friends, I'd end up serving at banquets and Christmas parties. By ninth grade, he made me do bookkeeping. I remember this one time when I had been doing the monthly journal, and I came out a penny short. Wouldn't you know that my father made me spend hours finding that penny?" She grins wide in reminiscence.

As host, chef, concierge, waiter, manager, fireworker, and architect, her father gave the hotel an overhaul around 1977 by removing the main staircase, throwing out the switchboard, and converting the lobby to his main office to conduct the growing pyrotechnics business, though he kept the restaurant, which is still in operation today. "The restaurant," interjects Donnalou, "was the family hangout. I used to love to eat pasta there, which I called 'sketti.' We did go out for Thanksgiving dinner, but my father hated it. We had to promise him that in return we'd have Christmas at home. He really is a true family man. He'd work very hard, come home for dinner, and then take us all out later for Dairy Queen ice cream."

Donnalou recalls that her father had always remained close to his family even when the fireworks business grew dramatically, which started right around the time of the hotel's conversion. Zambelli Internationale wasn't as international then as it is today; back then, George had his hands full just fulfilling domestic contracts. She explains that her father was always doing business, even on family vacations, and that he made a point of taking his family to see his shows near home, again combining work with business. Donnalou describes what her siblings also reiterate in telling how George Sr. would pile the family into the auto—with some of the children sitting on the floor of the car—and drive to Harrisburg, Atlantic City, or a legion of other places, where the family would

*Donnalou oversees her sisters at the pool. Annlyn poses on the edge of the pool, Marcy stoops in the water, and toddler Danabeth nuzzles up against her oldest sister.*

frolic on the beach while George was inside somewhere recruiting new business. "We did that so much," remembers Donnalou, "that my mother became an expert packer. She could get the belongings of all seven of us into nooks and crannies in suitcases that you never knew existed. She could pack fast, too. Even today, she's still packing."

When not on the road, the Zambellis stayed home and participated in school and community activities. On reflection, Donnalou envisions her father sitting in the audience, watching countless recitals, attending endless homecoming games. Luckily for George that at one time the four Zambelli sisters danced together, which helped cut down on recital attendance. "But no matter how busy my father was, he always came to our school events. He put a high priority on family activities, even if the family business got overwhelming," she says. "And holidays always held preeminence with him. This was family time, and we were expected to be together, especially at Christmas. Mom shopped for all of us . . . imagine buying gifts for five children, and a husband who didn't even remember what color socks he put on in the morning."

Smiling, she adds, "Every year, we got a new Christmas tree. One year, we convinced Dad to cut down a fresh one at the fireworks plant. It was huge! We had put it up, decorated it with love and finesse, and stood back and admired it. Smiles widened on our faces as we stood in admiration of our work. Then we filed out of the room, our exquisitely lighted tree behind us illuminating the house. From the next room, we heard a loud, shattering crash . . . and the rest can be figured out."

## Dad's Antithesis

While George Sr. figured as the disciplinarian to the children, Connie served as their friend and ally, disciplining with gentleness and tact.

"My mother was my best friend, and I'm sure my sisters would say the same thing. When I was young, she used to go with me to check out guys," laughs Donnalou. "My friends would come, and she'd use the kitchen as a launching pad for sandwich-making and ten-course meals. My friends loved her. Even today I talk to her daily, tell her all my problems. My mother worries a lot about being fair to all her children. Our whole family is like that; we all look after each other, protect one another."

Ironically, though, it was George Sr. who Donnalou went to when she had "real major problems. I remember being in Geneva College and having some concerns about my future. I got on the phone and called my father and cried. On the phone, Dad said, 'What's the matter, honey?' I told him. And although it wasn't anything significant in my life then—though I thought it was the end of the world at the time—he dropped everything he was doing and drove to the college to take me out for coffee just so I had a shoulder to cry on. I rambled on through tears, and he listened. To him, nothing was more important than his being there for me. I still remember that. He was there for me, too, when I was pregnant and nauseated with morning sickness. To me, those kinds of things say a lot about him."

To Dentist Zambelli, her father is just a good old-fashioned Italian man who in the end does what he wants, hears only what he wants, and thinks what he thinks is right. This includes his traditional philosophy that family always comes first, that a marriage is important, and that it's respectful to visit deceased loved ones at the cemetery on a regular basis. "He still does that—goes to his parents' and siblings' graves," says Donnalou, "and he takes his grandchildren with him, who seem to think it's a great jaunt with Papa."

Donnalou offers that her father disliked fighting among his children, even though that was as natural as whipped cream on pumpkin pie. "My father tended to overreact when any of us fought. Overall we all got along, though I do remember Marcy and I having one big fight, which is pretty much out of character for me, since I'm more of a 'yes' person. But most of the time we girls fought with our brother, which was a lot more fun than fighting among ourselves. My brother was pretty clueless about life . . . like most men." She laughs in a light, casual way that

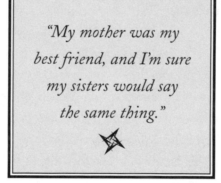

*"My mother was my best friend, and I'm sure my sisters would say the same thing."*

*George Sr. with his women attending one of many international fireworks conventions. Left to right: daughter Donnalou, wife Connie, George Sr., and daughters Danabeth and Marcy.*

entrances the listener, while giving her brother a quick glance and a smile. He smiles back from his table, where he periodically stabs the air with his fork to emphasize something to his father.

## A Role in the Business

Donnalou sips from her water glass, and motioning with a nod of her head towards her brother, she whispers, "My brother's just like my father—old fashioned in many ways, and always wanting to conduct business no matter where he is."

"Without a doubt, my father works too hard. He needs to slow down and enjoy life more. The only time I ever see him let go a little is when we take family cruises. The first two days on ship, he doesn't mention the word 'fireworks'; by the third, he's talking about them. By the fourth, we can all see how high-strung he's getting, which increases with each passing day. On the final day of our last cruise, he looks out the little porthole and mutters, 'Can't this ship go any faster?'" She laughs, recalling the incident. "My brother is almost as bad. Even with his hectic eye practice, he's still very involved in the family fireworks company. I suspect he'll continue to be, and perhaps even more so at some point in the future. I know I want to be."

Donnalou has done just that—got more involved with the family company—though she spends much time maintaining her busy dental

practice, located on the third floor of her father's hotel. She says, "One of the things I now do more of is travel to meet clients for my father. I've always been there for my parents. Now that my daughter Amberlee, 21, a chemistry major, is planning on attending dental school, I'm hoping she'll come into my practice and help ease my patient load. But I do serve as a consultant to and a representative of our fireworks company, and I attend conventions, take clients to dinner, and give input where I can."

She says, "When I first started taking a more active role in the business, I used to drive to Pittsburgh International Airport to meet clients and dine them, but when they'd see me, they'd say, 'You don't look like George.' They were really disappointed that my father wasn't there." Speaking of her father and airports, Donnalou says, "My dad is the only person in the world who can drive to the airport in record time. One time, my daughters Summer and Amberlee were riding to the airport with him. He drove like a dragster, making Summer barf in the car." She giggled schoolgirl style, bringing out that delightful smile of hers.

## The Business

**D**r. Donnalou Zambelli glances around the large private room in the Sheraton where there is a constant din of glasses clinking, forks scraping plates, and voices ringing low and high in the air. She looks pensive before saying, "This is what life is all about—family. I have a wonderful one. I'm pleased with how my parents raised us, proud of what my sisters Marcy and Danabeth do in Florida

> *"This is what life is all about—family. I have a wonderful one. . ."*

for the company, and equally proud of my other siblings. My children are my life. I have spectacular daughters who, I suspect, will some day get involved in fireworks just as everyone else in the family has. All the grandchildren have been raised on the staple of booms and bangs—just as my brother, sisters, and I have been; they'll become the inheritors of what my grandparents and parents have taken decades to build. Fireworks are so second-nature to the family that no one frets about whether there will be accidents. Thankfully," she adds, "Zambelli has an excellent safety record. We've had few mishaps, and none has been serious. The most recent occurred in October 1997 when one of the magazines at our English Avenue plant blew up. Luckily, we used that plant only for storage. When I heard it blow, I froze. All kinds of thoughts raced through my mind. Then I got a call from one of the major television stations." Donnalou instantly left her picture-perfect rambling home and got into her car, driving the short distance to her parents' house.

"'Dad,' I said to my father. 'One of the bunkers exploded.' The first thing out of his mouth was, 'Did anyone get hurt?' I told him no, and I could see the tension visually leave his face. 'That's what counts,' he added. He was very calm then, asking questions of logistics: how it had happened, how much damage had been done, and so on. I told him I didn't know but that some of the store windows downtown had shattered from the force. 'We'll take care of it,' he told me, while repeating, 'But you're sure no one's hurt?' I again reassured him. That's all that matters to my father because everyone at Zambelli Internationale is 'family,' even if they aren't related. We greatly value all our workers, who are more like

brothers and sisters to us than staff and crew. And my father cares as much about the New Castle community as he does about his employees." The people in the community have watched him build the company into the hallmark it is today.

Having finished her meal, Donnalou turns around in her seat and looks at her parents. A smile crosses her face. "I'm lucky to have them as my mother and father."

# The Daughters

### *Amberlee (Zambelli) Drespling*

Having finished their meals, both Amber and Summer bounce over to their mother, each wearing their trademark berets. One says to Donnalou, "We'd like to go down to the Point now, so we'll be there when we shoot off the fireworks."

Donnalou looks at her gorgeous, blond-haired girls and nods, giving the usual maternal caveats. Both girls are personable and mature beyond their youth. Their smiles are much like their mother's, and they possess her poise and style.

Amberlee says with a twinkle in her eyes, "I love fireworks! No matter how many times I see them, I still get excited. For me, it's like seeing them for the first time all over again. I enjoy traveling to the different shows we do, attending conventions, and meeting clients. I've had to learn how to act adult-like because I'm around clients a lot. Our whole family is required to play the proper host or hostess to my grandfather's customers. He expects us to be cultured, as well as savvy about protocol. Since we were raised on fireworks, my cousins, sister, and I know the business; it's never boring."

As is true with their Uncle George and Aunts Marcy, Danabeth, and Annlyn, both Amberlee and Summer have worked for their grandfather part-

time throughout the school year. Amber's jobs have ranged from filing, opening and dating mail, and faxing and photocopying to handling calls. She clarifies, "When I became sixteen, I turned into my grandfather's gofer. He has me driving here, running there, going to the airport to pick up clients. And he makes me wear these signs at Pittsburgh's huge airport so that clients can recognize me. How embarrassing! I've learned how to play the 'airport paging' game with his customers who seem to escape me when they come down the ramp. I can't complain because Papa's always there for me. If I'm troubled, he'll stop what he's doing and talk to me. He even went to my piano recitals. He's both sensitive and strict. If he thinks I've done something wrong, he'll lecture me, but when it's time to play, he's fun."

Amber, who wants to become a dentist, says her grandfather is distinctly different from her grandmother. "Even my friends visit my grandmother and tell her their problems. She always reassures me, makes me feel that I'm okay and that things will work out. Her famous words are, 'Fate will take its place.'"

While Grandmother Connie might be different from her serious husband, Amber knows her grandfather can be a "trip," too. She reflects, "This one time when I was out with him I happened to notice a couple of cute guys. My grandfather saw me checking them out, and doesn't he walk right up to them and say, 'I have a beautiful granddaughter; want to meet her?' I was so humiliated. I said to him, 'Papa, why did you do that!' He looked at me and grinned that charming smile of his, saying, 'Hey, if you want to get ahead in life, you have to take the initiative.'"

Is she going to take the Zambelli initiative? Amber admits that at some point she wants to be active in the company. "I think there will always be

someone in the family involved in the company. There are enough of us. It's a unique business. My friends think it's cool that we shoot fireworks, and that we're such a close family." She explains that one of the reasons the family is so close-knit is that they share a commonality and the pride that goes along with working hard: "When we're all standing and watching one of our shows, a sense of love fills each of us, because it's 'ours.' We smile at one another, knowing we're sharing something special."

### Summer Joy Drespling Wise

A graduate of Westminister College, Summer is a mirror image of her young sister Amber. She is the wife of Dr. Chad Wise, her mother's associate in her dental practice, whom she married on May 29, 2001. Perky, with shiny eyes and a bright smile, Summer claims, "I will never say that I've seen some fireworks show a thousand times, because no two displays are alike. I love the shows but I do want to have a professional life as well. So like my mother, I'll have my own career, but I'll always be a part of the family company. There's so much to learn about fireworks, and we're such a large corporation that there are enough places in it for all of us. I'm just grateful that the business has allowed me to see so much at my age. We've traveled all over the world, and I've experienced so much."

When asked how she would characterize her world-famous grandfather, she laughs her mother's laugh, shakes her head. "He's wonderful; I love him so much. At the same time, he can drive anyone

*"You know, there's a certain connection in our family. We're very tight-knit. And no one's worried about who's going to get what in the business. We know we'll all work together as a family unit. . ."*

nuts. He doesn't think people have lives other than 'fireworks.' He's very stern, expects things done *his* way, and thinks the world revolves around him and fireworks. I make sure I keep my distance from him come July 4th." She smiles, looks at her grandfather, then turns back and adds, "Papa is an energetic person, and a fantastic businessman. He teaches me a lot, tells me I have to learn to be tough in life, and yet he's gentle in many ways. Still, he can be the most frustrating person I know. I often work at corporate headquarters helping out my aunt (Annlyn) and there have been times where he's just driven me crazy. I've walked out of the office, saying, 'I can't handle this! He knows I'll get done what he wants.'

And then when I turn back around to look at him, my grandfather has that certain look on his face that just melts you."

Summer tries to figure him out. "He's a paradox, which I think contributes to his mystique. One day he joined the younger grandchildren in dribbling a basketball; another time, we were at a restaurant and from his seat he saw a guy smoking while sitting at the bar. He got up from his chair, went over to the fellow and took him outside where he lectured him on the evils of cigarettes and told him to stay outside and damage his lungs, and not smoke inside." Summer laughs at the memory. "To know my grandfather is to truly love him."

She adds, "This one time, while we were out, I told him, 'Papa, I'm really stressed out; college is so hard for me.' He looked at me tenderly, and sweetly said, 'We'll do whatever we can to get you through.'"

Summer exchanges a look with her mother before adding, "And my grandmother is just as great. I've traveled with her since I was four years old. She's so important to me. I think each of her children and other grandchildren would say the same thing. She's the peacekeeper in the family—very loving, very devoted to Papa and the rest of us. Do you know that when I took my school exams she was going to sit with me during my six hours of testing . . . just to be there for me? She's incredible." As an afterthought, she says, "I guess she'd have to be to live with Papa for fifty-some years." Summer explains that the theory of opposites attracting illuminates why her grandparents love each other so much. "My grandmother has always supported him. She'll come into the office to answer phones, talk with clients, or just keep Papa focused."

Before leaving to head down to the Point at Three Rivers to see the fireworks, Summer turns back and inserts, "You know, there's a certain connection in our family. We're very tight-knit. No one's worried about who's going to get what in the business. We know we'll all work together as a family unit. Even now, all the cousins try to spend time together, and we four oldest girls constantly talk to each other and go places together, even though we each attend different schools."

She pauses a moment, then tosses out one final thought. "No one has to tell me what a great family I have." With a sweep of her arm, she says, "This Christmas we all agreed to forfeit our family gift exchange and instead give that money to charity."

She winks at her mother, then exits with her sister and cousins, their voices high and excited at the

*Donnalou's dental office is in the Zambelli Building. Her family, left to right: Summer, Dr. Chad Wise (Donnalou's associate in practice), Connie, George, Amberlee, Dr. Donnalou, and husband Pat McVay. Pat has an important role in the Zambelli business.*

prospect of seeing their next display of fireworks.

Donnalou has married Pat McVay who works in the family business like all other "Zambelli" members. She pushes her plate away, and rises. Everyone in the private dining room is talking about the upcoming night's fireworks extravaganza. The tenor in the room is one of euphoria. "This is my family," says Dr. Zambelli. "I love them. We're a team."

The team leaves in unison to present one of the best shows they've ever given.

# FOUR

# Marcy Zambelli

## VICE PRESIDENT OF MARKETING

I
T'S THE EYES of the long-black-haired beauty that instantly cast a spell on you the second you meet her. Then, when Marcy Zambelli smiles at you, you know you have her undivided attention as her gaze pierces into you. The slender, former Miss Pennsylvania in the 1976 U.S.A. Pageant has an all-encompassing demeanor that conveys to others how competent she is, how well she takes control and conducts not only herself but an entire roomful of people as well.

In their Florida home, gorgeous daughter Aubriana pats her mother's elbows, wanting to share her mother's lap with her little sister Alandra, born December 6, 1997. Both are a handful for Marcy, who tries to run a house with two rambunctious young ones, as well as direct a major division of her father's fireworks empire. Aubriana Paige, who loves to play basketball and roller hockey, shares her mother's love for fireworks, and often visits her office and helps her choose the programs' music. Her little sister Alandra Noelle enjoys bike riding and playing dolls with her cousins. But she, too, goes to her mother's office to help pick out all those "pretty colors" that fireworks are made of. Both girls accompany their mother on business trips to learn more about fireworks. Marcy's grateful to her supportive husband Oscar Fumagali, the Chief Financial Officer for a major multinational telecommunications company. Says Marcy, "We balance out one another in juggling careers and kids. He's an extremely good father, too."

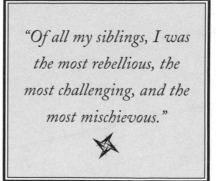

*"Of all my siblings, I was the most rebellious, the most challenging, and the most mischievous."*

Living in the Boca Raton area is quite a hike from her parents, who would have gladly babysat their grandchildren had they not been separated by more than 1200 miles. "It's hard being so far apart, but Mother gets down here quite a bit, and my father does his best to fly in to see the girls. He was amazing with our new baby, feeding her, patting her on the back to burp her. And he was so gentle with her. When he wasn't with Alandra, he was down on the floor playing with Aubriana." Marcy adds that during the times her dad is with her children, his entire being is focused on them, wanting to be a part of their world, to share with them, to let them know how much he loves them; on the other hand, he seems reflective of his life, as though he is of a designed past while they are of a random future. Though they may be of opposite poles, she senses that a part of each will somehow converge, somehow touch one another in a forever memorable moment.

"Let her cry," George Sr. tells Marcy on the phone, regarding his infant granddaughter who is wailing for food, attention, warmth. "That won't hurt her. It's good for babies."

"Daddy," Marcy contests, "you can't let a newborn cry. They do that for a reason."

"It never hurt you," George snaps back. "And you were my 'cries-a-baby,' always crying, crying."

Marcy laughs at the old nickname he had given her, while countering, "I was just sensitive." She says she still is but goes to great lengths to hide it. As a child, the more her sensitivity brought tears to her eyes, the more her father agitated her. One time he had made Marcy so tearful, she took handfuls of Saltine crackers, crumbled them, and spilled them on his head. "He sat there laughing at me," she says.

At other times, she catches her father indulging the grandchildren, and she has to remind herself that this is the same man who said, "Let the kid cry." Marcy says, "While there are times when my father looks as if he's fearful of squeezing my daughters, I've also seen him scoop them up into his arms and smile and coo at them. I think, even after twenty-some years, he's still trying to figure out this grandfather thing." She smiles. "He was probably like that with me, too."

# Childhood

**B**orn October 12, 1955, Marcy Zambelli comments, "I think I have my father's personality, though I'm less gruff and better looking. I'm the middle child—between the two older ones, Donnalou and George, Jr.—and the two younger ones: Annlyn and Danabeth. So I came equipped with all the hangups and traits of the middle-child syndrome. Of all my siblings, I was the most rebellious, the most challenging, and the most mischievous."

*Marcy evaluates one of her favorite shows in Mahoningtown, Pennsylvania where the famous Italian traditional fireworks doll dance occurs.*

But reserved Marcy was not. While Donnalou was obedient and immediately did what she was told, Marcy would stand her ground and argue with her father over his mandate. "He'd say, 'Go sit down,' and Donnalou would run to a chair, but I would stand my ground, look him in the eyes, and ask, 'Why?' I'm sure it's payback time with my kids," she laughs. "But my father would stare me right down until I did what he said. He was strict, and I knew just how far I could go. He yelled a lot. My mother, though, was his opposite, disciplining us with a steady, even tone that could lull you to sleep. We did what my mother wanted because she was tender about her demands, while with my father, we did what he wanted because we were afraid not to. He was a very stern, old-fashioned Italian father who expected his children to listen, even if you had a mind of your own. Yet, for as severe and headstrong as he was, he was just as loving. He made me feel secure around him, even if he did work a lot. I can remember going to Mahoningtown County's Italian festival and having hot sausage sandwiches with him. I felt so proud to be with him, and I basked in his smile and attention."

Ultimately, she would have to toe the line when he barked out orders. "We knew that if we did something wrong, there would be a consequence to pay." It was often during those times that Marcy grew closer to her sister Annlyn, who was fifteen

She describes her brother as having been funny while growing up—"He still can make me laugh," she says—and her older sister, Donnalou, as having been "the perfect child. If any parent ever wanted a child who did and said everything right, who excelled in everything, who could explain $e=mc^2$ as well as play piano, then Donnalou was that child. It's too bad humans couldn't have been cloned back then. There would have been a run on my sister's version." Speaking of prototypes, Marcy believes that Donnalou served "as a role model for me; I wanted to be just like her: intelligent, versatile, beautiful, reserved."

months younger than her. "Annlyn and I would try to think up ways to get around my father. We were inseparable; we played together all the time, dressed the same—like twins—did everything together, even shared the same bedroom. Annlyn was the rowdy one back then; she loved to party and take risks. And, of course, we fought at times, and when that happened, we'd draw an invisible line down the center of our bedroom and not let the other one cross over."

Marcy smiles at the fond memories, though she admits there are a few she'd like to erase much the same way chalk can be wiped off a blackboard. "Now, when I look back, those moments weren't so bad, but at the time they were horrendous, embarrassing, such as when my father would appear out of nowhere at one of our school dances. It was bad enough that he came to check out the dance and see if we were where we said we would be, but it was worse when he'd show up in a raincoat and hat. He went everywhere in that hat. That was the thing about my father: He'd show up at places you'd least expect, which is the reason we were always where we told him we would be."

Marcy says her father's sternness didn't prevent her from having friends. "My girlfriends loved him, thought he was 'cool,' because he had that charming way, and would spend time talking to them, teasing them. But my boyfriends were a different story. Whenever they'd see my father coming, they were like roaches in light, scrambling in all directions to get away. My father never yelled at them but he expected them to be gentlemen." She appends the memory with, "When my friends and I would be in the basement goofing off, my dad would come downstairs dressed in two different pairs of pajamas—the top maybe in plaids and the pants in stripes—and say to everyone, 'It's time you kids

went home.' And the more we'd tell him, 'Daddy, can't you dress right?' the more he did it to be humorous and embarrass us. He drove Annlyn and me crazy."

It was times like those—when George Sr. hassled Marcy and Annlyn—that the two sisters stuck up for one another, such as when they got blamed for calling in a false alarm to the fire department, and each defended the other.

If Marcy wasn't being yelled at by her father, then her older sister and brother were on her case. In the basement George Jr. and Donnalou would play records, and every time she and Annlyn would go down to join them, they'd get shooed away. "To this day, I can still hear in my head all the different songs Donnalou and Georgie played, like 'Blue Moon.' So Annlyn and I grew closer. We were as thick as thieves. When we were younger, Annlyn and I played dolls all the time. I remember when we had gotten a Barbie car—it was turquoise blue inside—and Annlyn and I pushed it up and down the street, laughing, pretending we were Barbie. Then we wrecked the little car into someone's porch step, and the two of us just sat down on the porch and cried into each other's arms." On reconsideration, Marcy offers, "All of us girls got Barbie dolls, and Donnalou has some of the originals. Well, she has the head of one original doll, but she's not sure about the body. She thinks her daughters—Amber and Summer—may have swapped bodies on her."

She and younger sister Annlyn grew tight. Marcy recalls how they had made dollhouses out of wooden crates, which was a lot more fun than playing with the type of fancy houses sold today. She grins in reminiscence of yore, adding what all her siblings have said countless times about how their father would drive the family to a city where he was to do business and then meet them later in the day to enjoy time together. "When we would be on an ocean boardwalk, he'd trip us kids because he thought that was funny; it was his way of kidding around." Likewise, she describes her version of how she and her brother and sisters would take their summer-night baths, get into clean pajamas, and wait on the front steps for their dad to come home from work and take them for ice cream or to McDonalds. "Such good recollections," she reflects.

"My mother would rise early, have coffee with my dad, and then we'd all breakfast together. On his way to the office, Daddy would drop us kids at school while Mom picked up rolls at a bakery to take to her parents' house, only to bring home the leftovers or a homemade waffle from my grandmother. My mom's like her mother was. My mother's father was quiet; he went to mass every morning."

Marcy says she felt connected to her father's parents, too, because her father was close to them. "Our whole family would go to Grandma Zambelli's every Sunday and watch 'The Wonderful World of Disney.' Except for my siblings and me, everyone spoke Italian, though my grandmother did speak broken English when talking to us. The house had this wonderful smell of homemade sauce. I loved it. Grandma Zambelli died when I was in the third grade; her funeral was the first I ever attended." Ironically, days after Antonio Zambelli had lain dying in a hospital bed, Connie Zambelli had lain in a hospital bed delivering her fourth child, Annlyn. Marcy says, "My father went in to see his dad, and Grandpa Zambelli asked him. 'Well, what did you have?' My father told him, 'A beautiful baby girl.' My grandfather said, 'That's good, George, because girls will always take care of you; you'll never be alone,' and then he died."

Some seven years later, the fifth child—Danabeth Zambelli—was born. Marcy remembers her father meeting her and Annlyn at their school on September 6, 1963, around noon, when they were en route to home for lunch. She had whispered to Annlyn, "Something big must be happening for Daddy to meet us at school." When they caught up with their father, he said, 'I have good news. You have a little baby sister.' Recalls Marcy, "We were so excited. After that, Danabeth became Annlyn's and my living baby doll. What sticks in my mind is how radiant my mother looked pregnant, making me aspire to motherhood.

"When Annlyn and I got a little older, we would go shopping on Saturdays, walking from our home into town—about two miles—and not think a thing of it. First, we'd stop at the office to ask my father for money. He'd say no right off, and then tell us to wait a few minutes. Pretty soon, he'd come by and hand us a couple of dollars, but he had to say no first. The last stop we'd make in town was to the florist where we always bought Mom a flower. Back then, the city neighborhoods were safe. You could walk around town, bike ride, play kickball with friends, and no one had to worry if you were safe. Today, you don't let your kids out of your sight." Marcy looks at her children. "It's only when you have your own children that you understand all those worries your parents had over you."

Did she worry her parents?

"Sure, but I was more shy when I was growing up than I am now. I even entered beauty contests to get out of my shell, such as Miss Sunburst and Miss Outer Space, where I painted my body silver and wore a multicolored wig. I remember when I won Miss Pennsylvania, and the MC asked me how I felt about it. I told him, 'I hope right now I'm a firecracker to my father.'" She laughs, making her babies smile with her. "All my life I wanted to please my father. I think I've accomplished that."

# Independence

By her late teens, Marcy and her father butted heads on a regular basis, making her think about leaving home and going away to college. She chose Marymount "in the boonies of Florida," she claims, explaining that she picked that school because her parents were in Florida a lot on business and this way she'd get to see them more than if she had gone to another college. Later, the name Marymount was changed to the College of Boca Raton, and now the school goes by the name Lynn University. A few years after Marcy arrived in Florida, her sister Annlyn followed her, and there the two sisters resumed their twin-like relationship.

But mobility proved to be a challenge at college. Marcy wanted a car and her father had promised her one. But he never came through. "So I rented one and sent him the thousand-dollar tab. He was not a happy camper." But then one summer, her dad had her filling out raffle ticket stubs for a charity organization. The prize was a car. She had so many to fill out that she wrote the names of all her family members, writing hers more than the others since she was the one needing transportation.

Marcy tells it best: "On July Fifth, a Sunday, our phone rang. It was a priest, which immediately spooked my father, who gave the phone to my mother. Mom listened, and then excitedly climbed the steps to my bedroom where she told me my ticket had been drawn and I had won a Chevy Nova. I was ecstatic! But my father traded it in for a safer car, getting me a Monte Carlo instead. I loved it; I drove it five years before I had to get a new one. I didn't know then that you had to have the oil changed, tires checked, get it washed and waxed, and all that stuff, so I pretty much drove it into the ground. So much has gone on in my life in

*Marcy as "Miss Pennsylvania" in the 1976 Miss U.S.A. Pageant, dressed as a firework. Her mother Connie made the costume so that the fireworks would light up in the dark. Marcy, who won the contest, says, "The outfit was heavy to wear but worth it."*

that automobile; if only that car could talk."

And if it could talk, it would tell about Marcy's partying. While Connie claims her daughter Marcy was the party girl, Marcy is quick to point a finger at Annlyn. "My sister was the wild, crazy one, not me," counters Marcy. "She'd go up to guys and say, 'Are you married?' and if they said no, she'd drag them over to me. That's how I met my husband, Oscar Fumagali. He was standing behind us in line at a grocery store when Annlyn approached him. He and I dated five years before we got married. I was quiet in college until Annlyn came. We'd do the nightclub scene at night, with one of us driving and the other doing our homework."

Even with partying, the two sisters did well in college. Marcy majored in sociology to become a social worker, though she suspected that at some point she would take on a career in her father's company. "I knew I wanted to work for my dad, even when women weren't yet entirely accepted into the business world." She, like all her siblings, had done time in George Sr.'s office, spending summer after summer photocopying, answering phones, filing—all during an era when, Marcy recalls, "fireworks were allowed to be transported in the trunk of your car; now, there's all those regulations."

Over time, she learned about those regulations, as well as how the company operates. Having worked in the corporate office while in high school and during summers off from college, she also visited clients in various cities, even if it was only to say hello on her father's behalf. Still, Marcy wasn't a full-time Zambelli employee, and wanting to become a top businesswoman was a major part of her life's goal, which she began to put into motion. But another part of her would surface, reminding her of how glorious her mother had looked during her pregnancy. "So I also wanted to be a wife and mother at the same time," says Marcy, who's been

> *"I knew I wanted to work for my dad, even when women weren't yet entirely accepted into the business world."*

juggling both ever since, just as she juggled college and a modeling career for Barbizon.

George Sr. had imprinted for her a life she had come to identify with. "I observed him. I never underwent formal training to become a business executive, but I learned from him, and argued with him from time to time. There have been many instances when I threw files on the floor in frustration. I'm his only employee who quit thirteen times but never once got fired. Once I got so mad that I quit and came back to Boca Raton to work for IBM. I figured I'd show my father that other employers could appreciate me. Well, I hated it. I really wanted to be in the family business, so without asking my dad, I opened a Zambelli Fireworks branch here. Having worked enough for him over the years, and watched how he did business, I knew what had to be done, so I got on the phone and called organizations and tried selling fireworks to them. My father was dubious, adhering to his philosophy that people should first prove themselves. I did that. I made sales, handled the contracts from here, and soon I was running this office in correlation with headquarters. In fact, I was doing so well that my sister Annlyn came down to help but moved back to headquarters to be with our father. Then Danabeth relocated here to work with me. Now our father calls me for advice on things and thinks nothing of dropping major accounts in my lap, expecting me to handle chief marketing decisions."

She smiles, adding, "My family doesn't make a big deal about titles because we're one unit functioning together for a common goal. But when I'd

work with clients, they'd ask for my business card, wanting to know what position and authority I had in the company to make decisions. So I dubbed myself vice president of marketing." Even though she's proven herself over and over again, there are moments when her father disagrees with her. "And ninety percent of the time, he's right," she concedes, "but the other ten percent, I'm right, even though he won't always admit it."

## The Company and Its Future

**M**arcy comments that in many ways her father has been lucky that he has children who love him and want to continue his efforts, as well as a wife who has given him the space he needed to succeed, along with her support and personal efforts in making his success happen. She says, "Mom's always been the woman behind the scenes, but believe me, without her, I don't think our company would be where it is today."

And where it is today—world renowned, one of the biggest among them all—is the same place it will be tomorrow, according to the family's intentions. "I'm uncertain of what's in store for Zambelli Fireworks Internationale," begins Marcy, "other than the company continuing to exist to make people happy, and family members remaining at the helm. My dad is getting older now, though he remains a veritable ball of energy, but at some point I think he'd like to slow down enough to enjoy these years with my mother. The problem is that none of my siblings or I—working as individuals—could replace him; it would take all of us together to equal one George Zambelli Sr. He's a unique person. He loves his work, his employees, and his customers. Some company presidents claim they're there to help consumers, but my father *is* truly there for

*Marcy confers with her father, George Sr. over a major Fourth of July fireworks celebration in West Palm Beach, Florida.*

them, to make them happy. At fireworks shows, he makes a point of not only watching the display, but also of analyzing people's expressions to see if they liked what they saw, what he could change to make it better. He tries to determine if his shows have made them worry-free and thrilled, if only for a few minutes. Typically, he'll walk around a display site after one of our shows and ask total strangers if they liked the show. He wants to make sure he's bringing joy to others, as well as instilling in us the value of giving personal attention, of treating customers the way we'd want to be treated."

Marcy adds that her father is the type of man

*Aubriana, Connie, George holding Alandra, Marcy, and husband Oscar Fumagali, who is the CFO of a multinational company.*

who would drop everything in a second if someone—friend, family, or even foe—called and asked for help. "That's just the way he is. He prizes people, and he's passed that down to his children. He especially treasures his employees, whom he treats like family members. They all understand him and, in spite of his compelling drive and occasional rigidity, they love him as much as he loves them. My father's not the type of person to show his affection, but we all know how grateful he is to his staff, whom he credits for helping him get where he is today."

Marcy likes the idea of having two daughters because she believes they'll grow close, just as she and her other three sisters have. "My brother is special to us, but there's a certain bond sisters have that doesn't exist with brothers. Because my parents had four daughters, Zambelli Fireworks will fare better for it. We'll all look to my brother if something should happen to my father, but we girls will have a primary role in the company, too—a role that allows

us to work in unison and not be cutthroat over who's in charge, and who's doing what or getting what. Females are less competitive than men about such things; they see the big picture and will strive to get the job done, whether large or small."

Marcy says, "Zambelli Fireworks is always ready for any celebration; it's exciting."

Aubriana lifts herself up to whisper into her mother's ear, "I love you." Marcy issues the same back, kissing her daughters, both of whom are adopted. She comments, "I always say that Grandma Thomas—my mother's mother—helped me to find my two babies." She looks at both and grins that maternal smile understood only by children, and adds, "Isn't that what life's all about? Being here for others? My parents taught us that. Do you see how much we owe them? Maybe it's not my father who's the lucky one after all; maybe it's my brother and sisters and me."

She turns back to her girls and reenters that private world of mothers and children.

*Marcy and Aubriana share the joy of Alandra's Christening day.*

# FIVE

# Annlyn Zambelli

## EXECUTIVE ASSISTANT

S ITTING IN THE WAITING ROOM of her father's headquarters, taking a rare break, Annlynn Zambelli reflects on her past and assesses her future. She claims she has two purposes in life: to serve her family and always be there for them, and to help her father and be there for him as much—a tough job to do when both are demanding and time-consuming.

Says the fourth of the five Zambelli children, "My husband and kids are my priority. I live for them, and spend every minute I can with them." (Her son Michael was born in 1989 and daughter Constance in 1992.) Just as devoted as she is to her family, she's that dedicated to her father. "I'm crazy about him," she confides. "Daddy's an outstanding businessman, a wonderful father, and a remarkable grandfather. No matter how tied up he is with corporate affairs, he always makes time for his grandchildren, just as he did when my sisters, brother, and I were growing up. That's why I like to be here for him."

Annlyn tells how excited her son and daughter become when they're with their grandfather, as most recently, when in a restaurant, George put Michael next to him, and, oblivious to everyone, handed him a pen so the two could play "boxes" on a paper napkin. A grin as wide as the sky spread over George Sr.'s face, and his entire being focused on this young man who someday might, himself, be focused on the company. "Aw, Michael," the grandfather said, "you cheated; no fair," and he shook his head and laughed. Then he doted on little Constance.

"Papa," said the light-complexioned, curly-haired tot, "I want to play in the snow."

George Sr. glanced out the restaurant window and shrugged. "Okay. We'll go together." Minutes later he excused himself, pulled on his trenchcoat and—in his suit and dress shoes—went out into the cold, windy night and obliged his grandchildren.

"That's why they love him so much," confirms Annlyn. "He never thinks about himself."

## Growing Up a Zambelli

Annlyn Zambelli fondly recalls her childhood years when her father would leave the office to attend her dance recitals and cheerleading events, or to meet with her teachers, along with chauffeuring her and her friends around. She doesn't remember any time when her father wasn't busy or trying to build the fireworks company. Yet he would make lunch and dinner with the family, no matter how engaged he was with a client or an office project.

"My father was conscientious about sharing his time with us. I can still envision how he used to pile us in the car to meet a customer. Lots of times it was at amusement parks, since they were a major part of our clientele. When we went to places where there was a beach, Mom would watch us in the water while my father conducted business. When he was done, he'd join us. Clearly I can see him, at the end of a long work day, walking on the sand toward us, throwing himself into the water and jumping waves with us, laughing, relishing every minute with his wife and children." She smiles, adding, "But he was just as strict as he was loving."

Annlyn—the shyest of all the siblings—recalls how her father had certain ideas on how children should be raised, such as not speaking unless spoken to and making sure everything on the plate was devoured before being excused. "You know the routine," she says, "some starving kid in some strange-sounding country. He made us appreciate what we had."

This tightly connected family grew up trusting and relying on one another. "We'd do anything for each other. I identified more with my sister Marcy, who's closest in age; we were really close. But we argued, too, like all sisters did."

Annlyn shares her memories of Christmas at home, relating how the entire family traditionally got the tree, set it up, and trimmed it—among carols, gaiety, and laughter. The next morning, Dad and Mom would be awakened early by squealing children eager to go downstairs and open presents. George Sr. would make his five children sit at the top of the stairs while he set up the camera; Connie would put on a pot of coffee and throw something together for breakfast. When their father yelled, "Okay!" the five would scramble down the steps, whooping and roaring, and dive head first into their presents. Annlyn hopes to pass this family tradition on to her children. She says, "Same thing: On Christmas morning, I'm making the coffee while Michael runs the video camera of Constance and little Michael opening their gifts. We've always taken photos and videos of our kids, from the

*The Zambelli women at the world's largest fireworks display, "Thunder Over Louisville," presented by Zambelli Fireworks Internationale. From left to right: Marcy, second oldest daughter; mother Connie; Danabeth, youngest daughter; Donnalou, oldest daughter; and Annlyn, third oldest daughter.*

moment they were born to this very day. After all, it's the only way to preserve memories."

Just as the family preserve memories, they also preserve their religious observances, especially at Christmas. Explains Annlyn, "For our family, church attendance was mandatory. Every Sunday we'd go to mass, and my siblings and I would attend Sunday School. After, we'd get hot bread and visit my grandparents for dinner, where we'd eat and eat. In the spring, my dad's mother would give us tulips to take home. She always gardened. We were a typical Italian-Catholic family."

In the spring, their father created another tradition—one all the children remember. When he'd complete his work at the office, he'd go home to his kids, who were dressed in their pajamas. But instead of putting them to bed, he'd put them in the car and take them out for ice cream. The hotel-restaurant business was as much an integral part of their tradition as were their ice cream forays and their fireworks business. Though Annlyn wasn't greatly involved in the restaurant, she enjoyed going there with her friends to eat 'meatball splashes.' "My friends loved the food as much as they loved my parents. Daddy would tease and agitate us while my mother would cook, making sure everyone was well fed. She even used to make food ahead of time just to have it on hand in case Dad brought home a business associate, a relative popped in, or one of our friends came over. Everyone thought she was the best cook."

The food wasn't the only thing her friends liked; they loved the fireworks, too. Before the Zambelli name became known internationally, Annlyn's

*Annlyn looks over the shoulders of Zambelli family members at corporate headquarters. Seated left to right: husband Michael, father George Sr., and mother Connie.*

friends thought it unique that the family lighted the skies for a living, while the New Castle community appreciated that Zambelli Internationale was and is one of the world's largest pyrotechnics company, and the only one that exhibits a voluminous number of shows annually.

"While we were growing up," says Annlyn, "some of our friends went with us to fireworks shows, and they would just be spellbound—not only at the fireworks display they watched, but also at what went on behind the scenes. They thought it was kind of neat that my entire family traveled around the world on business."

With both parents being so involved in business, the Zambelli children were expected to take on certain responsibilities. Annlyn and her siblings had to help out around the house, do what they were told . . . without whining, griping, slamming doors, stomping off. With their father, counter-arguments

weren't allowed. "And yet," laughs Annlyn, "he's more than indulgent with my children. He's the typical, authoritarian Italian father. By just a look or a grunt on his part, I'd shape up real fast. Even now I don't argue back with him, and I was a lot more outgoing then than I am now. My mom, though, was more calm."

As is true for her siblings, Annlyn, too, was the recipient of her mother's unending understanding. "Mom always took on Dad on our behalf. She just had a way about her that could get him to melt. She'd come to our defense when needed, and she spent an interminable amount of time with us. She was like my best friend, while my father was the boss of the family. What he said, went." One of the things her father said that "went" was that Annlyn was to go to college. "There was no alternative; my parents expected all of us kids to get a degree. Daddy was real big on education; good grades were important to him."

Annlyn followed Marcy to Florida, majoring in elementary education at Florida Atlantic; she had always wanted to teach in order to put her love for children to good use. Soon after graduating, she returned to New Castle to substitute teach in Pennsylvania schools. But her attraction to fireworks, and her desire to help her father in his growing company, made her change course and go into the family business for awhile. "Awhile" turned into years.

## At the Office

The office is a macrocosm of an ant hill, with people rushing here, carrying this or that, phones ringing from morning until quitting time, faxes whirring, photocopiers humming, and printers droning. There is never any downtime at Zambelli Internationale, and the Fourth of July—though a festive holiday for the family—can be a nightmare with nearly 2,000 shows on the docket. That's when every member of the Zambelli company willingly stays late to complete work, exerts extra energy, and gives more of themselves to fulfill all the jobs lined up for the patriotic holiday. George Sr.'s entire family doubles their efforts, including the classy Mrs. Zambelli, company vice president. "My mom's always giving of herself, trying to ease our loads. If it means babysitting my children to free me, she'll do it without a comment or a sigh. She's special," comments Annlyn.

Get busy, Annlyn does. As her father's aide, she's kept occupied filing this, fetching that, making phone calls, meeting with clients, writing reports and other papers, serving as a liaison for her father, comforting him when he's having an off day, organizing every minute detail that comes to his attention, and working with the entire staff. She says, "It can be very trying working for one's father and his staff, but I'd rather work for him than anyone else. He's demanding, but means well. Demanding is what got him where he is." Respect fills her eyes when she adds, "It's true that my dad's tough. He wants things done, and he wants them done yesterday. He expects that what he assigns others to do will be accomplished. I'm proud of him for what he has done for the family and his business, and I admire him for his salesmanship abilities, his way with people, his creativity. He's a miracle man, having built a small family enterprise into a large corporation that's known and esteemed all over the world. He's done a commendable job in providing us—his children and

> *"My mom's always giving of herself, trying to ease our loads. If it means babysitting my children to free me, she'll do it without a comment or a sigh. She's special."*

wife—with what we needed . . . and more. I wish I had half his energy. I do a lot in the office, taking all the steps to get to an end I've yet to see, but my father's incredible. It would take all my sisters and brother working together to equal his energy. He has to be a part of everything. I'd like to see him slow down, enjoy life, spend more time with my mother and his grandchildren."

While Annlyn's a whiz inside the walls of the main office, she's uncomfortable going out in public, preferring to remain behind the scenes—working with her father, handling all his minutiae, making herself available to help him in initiating sales. She feels her sisters do a better job in dealing with the public and are naturals at it. She has no desire to take control of the company and shepherd it through the millennium. She's happy just helping her dad and fixating on her children and husband. On reflection, she says, "In some ways my husband is like my father, but in others he's entirely different."

## A "Family Woman"

Her husband, Michael Richards, also works at Zambelli Internationale, as the Director of Operations. While George Sr. is hesitant in banking on modernized, newfangled methods, Annlyn's husband finds that he not only relies on them but that he *needs* them to get his job done. Computerization is Michael's forte in putting a show together or choreographing music and lasers to fireworks. So Annlyn deals with both her father

*Annlyn's family travels to many shows with her parents. She is her dad's right hand. Left: Connie, Annlyn, Michael Jr., and Constance seated on George Sr.'s lap.*

band." She shakes her head and giggles.

Michael became her husband after sister Danabeth introduced the two. Their year-long engagement reinforced their love for each other, and so in 1988, they united as one, holding their reception at Caesars Palace in Las Vegas. Of course, fireworks reverberated throughout the night in celebration. Shortly after, Michael got involved with Zambelli Internationale, toiling side by side with his wife and father-in-law.

To Annlyn, nothing is more important than building strong relationships, making herself available to her loved ones "just as my mother did," clarifies the long-blond-haired gal with the bright eyes and magnificent sense of humor. "It kills me to have to leave my children to go to work. Our son Michael Jr. [born in 1990] loves basketball and golf, and is very active in the family business, though his desire right now is to become an architect. Our daughter, Constance [born 1993] is a real performing-arts buff, and takes up ballet, tap, and jazz. She also likes soccer and golf. She'll play some role in our fireworks business, but now she's saying she wants to be a teacher. In the evenings, we spend time together, and weekends are devoted just to each other. I also take one day off from work every week to spend with Constance. My husband Michael is a gem. If I'm busy at work, he'll take the kids here or there, do dishes or grocery shop—whatever I need. My husband and I are so exhausted after getting off work that when we arrive home, it's all we can do to get dinner on, run the kids around, attend their events. We don't go anywhere . . . even on weekends. And if we have to travel, attend a fireworks or trade event, our children go with us. We thought nothing of carrying them, when they were babies, in wicker baskets to fireworks shows. After all, as my father says—we're a 'family' business."

and husband on a day-to-day basis in a family and in a business environment. She says, "It's good that our building is large enough to give my husband and me space, though I don't mind being with him all the time. We're both so busy that we don't spend a lot of time with each other. He has things to do, and Lord knows, I do, too."

Annlyn jokes that it's a wonder she got married at all since her father guarded his daughters like a Doberman over its property. George Sr.'s rule was that none of his girls was to be alone with a guy. For Annlyn and her sisters, it was difficult getting to know a young man with your father sitting nearby pretending to read a newspaper while one eye wandered to the couple sitting on the couch. "He was like that even when I was in my twenties!" exclaims Annlyn. "He wouldn't let me alone with Michael, who was going to be my hus-

*A 24-inch diameter shell dwarfs the Detroit skyline with a 2,400-foot spread. The shell below it (left) is a 12-inch.*

*Light Up the Night, Pittsburgh, December Holiday Celebration.*

*Coors Field, Colorado Rockies Baseball, Denver, Colorado.*

*ABOVE:* **Target Aquatennial Fireworks, Minneapolis, Minnesota.**      © Angel Art Ltd.

*RIGHT:* **Close proximity indoor fireworks and gerbs at the grand opening of the new Expo Center at the South Florida Fair and Expo Center, West Palm Beach, Florida.**

ABOVE: *Children's Hospital of Pittsburgh 2002 Field of Dreams Gala at PNC Park. Left to right: George, Jamie Lee Curtis, Connie, and Kevin McClatchy, owner, Pittsburgh Pirates.*

RIGHT: *Denver Broncos Football halftime show.*

BELOW: *Zambelli fireworks launch from 13 rooftops and a ground location in Las Vegas, New Year's Eve.*

ABOVE: *Zambelli fireworks at a Maryland fair.* © Angel Art Ltd.

RIGHT: *Talking hands and a fireworks tie reflect the excitement of George Sr. when he talks about his love for fireworks.*

## Dancing in the Heavens

**I**n a couple of rooms down from Annlyn's office, Michael Richards sits in his high-backed swivel chair, his fingers poised on a keyboard, his shoulder cradling the telephone receiver. The lanky, preppy-looking director of operations wows everyone with his computer skills in choreographing fireworks—an area he dove into many years ago. His face lights up and his eyes blink rapidly as his hands skim the computer keys the way a concert pianist lovingly caresses the ivories. "This is a program called 'Fire One,'" he says, adding that he helped develop it with a Penn State University company. For a pyrotechnics computer choreographer, "Fire One" is a dream come true, as it allows choreographers to select the type of shells they want to fire at the precise moment in a musical composition. The program keeps track of cost, inventory, and materials—tabulating all shell selections, what will be fired and when, and the burn time of fuses, as well as developing a script or log for packing. In essence, the program furnishes him with the ability to generate and execute an entire show.

It works this way: A computer—called the master console—is taken to a radio station in the area where a show is to be displayed. Michael programs it to time precisely with the show's music, which will be played stereophonically over the airwaves. A second computer (a remote console) is set up at the display site where it's connected by communications modules to the shells' squibs. These shells are numbered in sync with the script programmed by Michael, so that they will be fired precisely to a tenth of a second. The coordination among the master computer, remote console, and communications modules leading to the squibs is mind-boggling. But Michael makes it seem easy and fun.

Currently, he's giving his input on how to create a program that will allow an entire fireworks show to be previewed on the computer screen exactly as it will display on the night of the presentation. "I'm excited about this because clients will see what they'll get for their money before the actual show is fired. Thus they'll be able to make adjustments prior to the display—perhaps adding more shells, deleting others, redesigning set pieces, changing the music. This will be a real "boom" to our industry."

By his enthusiasm, one can see how much he loves his job.

> *Annlyn jokes that it's a wonder she got married at all since her father guarded his daughters like a Doberman over its property.*

## Mixing Business With Family

**B**y chance, Annlyn and Michael pass each other in the long hall of the office suite. They smile at each other but move along, needing to get to papers and mail piles, make calls to clients, listen to music to complement a show, design a set piece specific to a performance's theme, write a script for a display, or run to the plant to talk to a factory worker. Rarely do they talk shop much at home. They do so much of it at work that at home they prefer to concentrate on their private lives. Yet fireworks are so much a part of their day-to-day existence that there's hardly a moment when they're not involved in the art.

*Annlyn's husband Michael, and son, Michael Jr., listening to Q-tones in the final moments before Zambelli's exhibition for the Canton Hall of Fame show in Canton, Ohio.*

Reflects Annlyn, "We're such a busy corporation that often my husband takes work home. Our children see this, so we're providing a good work ethic for them while interesting them in the business. Constance loves fireworks; no matter how many times she sees them, she jumps up and down and talks about Papa's fireworks. Little Michael has expressed interest in the computerization end of the business, much like my husband. That's good, because then there will be another generation of Zambellis to run the company."

Annlyn relates how one night young Michael watched his father at the computer demonstrating the way "Fire One" can be synchronized accurately to the music. Suddenly, Michael Jr. bolted from his position of observation to his father's side, excitedly saying, "Here, Dad, play this CD; it goes better with the shells you've picked on the program." Michael the father, glanced down at his son, then returned to

concentrating on the computer screen. His brows furrowed, his fingers paused at the keys. "Try this CD, Dad!" the lad squealed again. "Hurry up, Dad!"

Annlyn sighed, saying, "That's the one phrase I dislike—'Hurry up!' My father says that to me. I hurry for him, give him what he wants, and then it takes him a week to get to it." She laughs. "But, boy, is it hard to get mad at him. My dad, who just has a way about him, is a real charmer, which is one of the reasons he's so successful. It's how he smiles, the way he pats your shoulder, that makes you melt. I just hope that some day I'll be as good with people as he is. My father's a very special man, and I love him dearly."

Annlyn proves this every day by going into the office and working with George Sr. She doesn't have to worry about becoming as special as her father . . . she already is.

# SIX

# Danabeth Zambelli

## VICE PRESIDENT OF SALES

S TANDING NEAR THE PASS-THROUGH WINDOW between her office and Marcy's, younger sister Danabeth could be mistaken for Annlyn's twin. To the undiscerning, it's difficult to tell the two apart, except by their laughter. While Annlyn's laugh is more subdued, sounding much like the crackling of ice in a glass, Danabeth's is almost raucous and overwhelmingly infectious, revealing a bit of her youthfulness as the last in line of the five Zambelli children. Although all of them have fared well in life, Danabeth enjoyed some advantages her siblings didn't.

## Childhood

S he explains, "I traveled with my parents from the time I was 15 months old. They took me everywhere: the World Series, conventions, royal palaces, and presidential homes. It was nothing to have breakfast in

Pittsburgh, lunch in Maryland, and dinner in West Virginia. I was with them so much that people thought I was an only child. My father's always had such a love for fireworks that he never seemed to get enough of them, even if they were his own. He even used to celebrate our birthdays with fireworks." So it wasn't unusual for her to be on the road moving from show to show, event to event, meeting people, doing unusual things— like riding in the official car of the Indy 500. Clients treated her royally, and throughout each meeting George Sr. reigned as potentate.

While Danabeth confesses that her father was strict, she adds that he enthusiastically took her to work with him at the hotel restaurant where he'd treat her to lunch. Even then, when just a kid, she could detect his devotion to pyrotechnics. "He was good at both the hotel and fireworks businesses. He just has an engaging way about him, a certain smile, a twinkle in his eyes. He's unique, and in some manner this is communicated to others. This is why he has the number of clients he has. And, gosh, is he a hard worker!" Though her admiration and love for her father is fluid and abundant today (she says that they are closer now than ever), she can remember her teenage years when she and her dad didn't always agree, even though by everyone's account Danabeth was a shy child who obeyed her parents.

She clarifies, "Mom disciplined in a tactful, tender way; my father yelled, except for those times he'd come home for lunch and wouldn't always talk." Danabeth adds, "My home was a hangout for my

friends, and when they'd see Daddy's black car come up the driveway, they'd jump on their bikes and ride off." She smiles, saying, "He'd tease them from the second he saw them until the moment they left. That was his way of saying he liked them."

And her father was an expert at knowing what he liked.

"My father stood by his beliefs, pure and simple. If he felt something wasn't good for me, even though I might be hurt by his decision, he remained unbending, no matter if I pouted, cried, or looked destroyed. Once he said 'no', that was it. Sometimes all he had to do was give me a look, as if staring at me from the top of his eyebrows; he still gives me that look when I do or say something that doesn't sit well with him. Or he lets out a low, rumbling grunt from the bottom of his gut, and I know he's reached his limit. I was never one to push him anyway; when 'enough was enough,' he was resolute, and I'd back off immediately. He was just very stern, but now, years later, I understand that he was that way because he loved his children and wanted only the best for us. My mother was, and is, the only one who can get around him. She knows him very well."

Danabeth can attest to this because, in her own words, she was her mother's shadow. "I grew up with Mom always being there." So while her father served as the disciplinarian, her mother ministered as best friend and confidant.

"Even to this day, I still ask her opinion. And in the end, she's always right. I should have listened to her in the first place when I was younger, instead of

> *"My father stood by his beliefs, pure and simple. If he felt something wasn't good for me, even though I might be hurt by his decision, he remained unbending, no matter if I pouted, cried, or looked destroyed."*

*Hours before the fireworks display for the Christmas program sponsored by President Jimmy Carter and First Lady Roslyn, Danabeth meets with her parents to pose and smile. World ice skating champion Peggy Fleming was a guest at this show.*

As a young girl, Danabeth had helped her mother get ready for those social affairs, even watched her mother cook for each of those events—preparing fabulous, elaborate meals. Yet Danabeth, who enjoys cooking, doesn't always have time to make homemade dinners because of the late hours she keeps at the office or the time she spends traveling for the company. She says, "Can you imagine being an Italian woman and not cooking every night?" She laughs her contagious laughter while adding, "It confounds Daddy that I don't cook as much as my mom. My father thinks all Italian women should be Julia Child in a Sophia Loren body."

Without a doubt, Danabeth's mother—Connie—is a thin, petite version of a Julia Child in her own right. She learned to cook from her mother, who, claims Danabeth, offered the same kind of bond Connie formed with her own children: "My mom and her mother were very close, just as my mother and I are. My mother is a warm, caring, giving person—like my grandmother was. Grandma Thomas cooked a lot, too." Granted, Danabeth got away with not cooking, and was deemed the "baby" of the family, but was she the perfect child?

"Of course, I was," she laughs, recalling an incident when she had gotten her sister Annlyn so angry at her that Annlyn let loose with a left and slugged Danabeth. Their father stiffened at the behavior of the two girls, and then, while pointing to the upstairs, he yelled, "Go to your bedroom and say the entire rosary for fighting!" Danabeth declares with

doing things my way and then having to admit later that Mom was right to begin with." The "being" with her mother while growing up not only formed a bond between them that was sealed forever, but it also offered Danabeth a heroine upon whom to model her life.

"My mother—my role model—was the perfect wife and mother, and the glue in our family. She was, and still is, my father's support. Our clients love her! No matter how crazy things get in the business, no matter how preoccupied she may be, she's always there for us children and my father. She's given us a sense of place and identity, as well as traditions and ideals to follow." Danabeth says, "I can remember how we all used to go to our grandparents for Sunday dinner after mass. Then, later, my mother had everyone over to our house for dinner, where her sparkling eyes reflected her joy for cooking. She cooked for nearly every party she and my father hosted, too."

that smirk on her face, "But it wasn't my fault."

In looking back, Danabeth muses, "My mother and father were good parents. I wouldn't change anything. People today say that they wish they could be a member of my family. I always tell them that anyone over forty could be adopted by my parents, but no one younger than I."

## Leaving Home

While in high school, Danabeth would help out in Zambelli Internationale corporate office on a part-time basis—answering phones, opening mail, typing, and photocopying—which carried over into summer work until she went to college. "In the Zambelli family, everyone worked in the fireworks business, and the older grandchildren do so even now. My father believed it was important, as a family, for all of us to have an understanding of the company's foundation as well as its superstructure. We learned this by working in all aspects of the company." With a smile, she adds, "But he never made me work in the plant; he was afraid I'd blow myself up and everyone with me. But he made it clear I had to get a degree."

With Danabeth, the phrase that best befits her is "bright child . . . bright future." She was one of those special kids who graduated a year early from high school because of her academic achievements. "I was pleased that I had attained good enough grades to graduate early, but in many ways I missed being with my classmates," says the perky lady whose intelligence nearly prodded her into considering law as a profession.

*"It confounds Daddy that I don't cook as much as my mom. My father thinks all Italian women should be Julia Child in a Sophia Loren body."*

"My brother became a doctor; my sister, a dentist. I didn't want medicine to be my career." She recalls her admission to the University of Maryland College Park—a school that has produced many well-known politicians, celebrities, writers, and others of note. There she majored in criminal justice with the intent of spending the next three years after graduation in a highly competitive law school. "I liked the university because it was a good school and yet close to D.C., although it took me a little while to learn my way around. One time when I was to meet my parents in the capital, I got lost for two hours motoring around its streets." She throws her head back and laughs.

After graduating from college, Danabeth went to Florida to visit her sister Marcy . . . and there she remained. For her and the other Zambelli children, Florida was a second home, especially after Marcy opened a company division in Boca Raton. "It felt right" to Danabeth, who had sunk her teeth into the fireworks business at Marcy's side and has savored it ever since.

"I love the work." She glances across the glass window at her sister. "Here, in the Florida office, is where we do much of the corporate consumer relations and marketing, as well as the management of various sales accounts." She says she doesn't miss not having gone to law school because what she's doing now seems natural to her: "While I'm cherishing my work," she begins, "I'm also helping my father." That's important to Danabeth, who feels that her parents have done so much for her that what she's doing for them now isn't a chore at all. She asks how something one loves can be a "chore" anyway. "The fireworks business is time-consuming, but it's also exciting and challenging, and requires not only substantial management skills but also a high degree of creativity. I think I'm using as much of my God-given talent doing this work as I would have had I become a lawyer, and the headaches are the same," she laughs.

One thing working in the pyrotechnics industry has done for her is eliminate the shyness that had eclipsed her throughout her elementary and high school years. Now she ventures out securely into the world—jetting here and there to meet clients, giving presentations, making sales, and relating to the public at large on the value of fireworks.

*The Zambelli family savors a quiet moment with Saudi Arabian Prince Bin sultan Bin Abdulaziz before a fireworks exposition. Left to right: Danabeth holding nephew Michael Jr., Annlyn, Summer (Donnalou's daughter), Connie, the prince, George Sr., and Melanie (George Jr.'s wife) holding son Jared.*

## In the Business

At the Boca Raton bureau, Danabeth—as vice president of sales—handles the big deals with Marcy, as well as the technicalities of the business. She chats with Marcy through the small sliding glass window where they hand papers back and forth, make major corporate decisions, discuss the workload of the many Zambelli workers, and even slip one another snacks when neither is keeping books, creating marketing campaigns, working with sales staff, writing reports, designing programs, or talking to clients. Both Danabeth and Marcy have such full days that each is exhausted by the time they get home late after office hours. But that they work well together and with all of the other company members helps them to achieve what's best for the corporation and its clients.

Says Danabeth, "It's great working with my sister. We click. Marcy's more of a 'big picture' kind of person, where I'm detail-oriented and well organized. I like taking care of particulars, such as bookkeeping and accounting, acquiring permits, managing the office, and overseeing sales—along with coordinating the California branch, which handles fireworks for the western region of the country. Marcy's more creative and broader in scope."

Danabeth's too modest. She's always there for Marcy, who needs assistance in managing the busy company's advertising, marketing, and sales. Their work requires constant traveling, obtaining insurance, attending conventions, creating proposals, performing site surveys, "and doing endless business over the phone, even though most of our accounts come from word-of-mouth," she interjects. "Our life is fireworks, and our name's on every single shell

*The family discusses a corporate marketing plan in George Sr.'s office at corporate headquarters. George and Connie are seated left, and Danabeth and Marcy are at the right.*

we shoot. We have always maintained an excellent record and will continue to do so. Our aim is to remain in the forefront of the industry simply because we care and work hard at what we do best."

One wonders if that's as true with the small shows that are in the $5,000 range as it is with the extravaganzas in the $100,000-plus realm. "You bet it is!" Danabeth emphasizes. "To us, all shows are *big* shows, no matter what the cost. We treat them equally, with the same amount of diligence, time, energy, and care. A small show requires the same amount of work as a big one does. For us, every show is like doing the first one, so we put as much into each presentation, no matter how major or minor."

Danabeth says the work is draining but not exhausting enough for her to give it up. "I want to continue with what I'm doing now. Oh sure, I'll make some adjustments, but I like my work, and I

love my life." Married to Gary Trasatti, she juggles fireworks with domestic life. "Sometimes people who aren't in the fireworks business don't always comprehend what we do, but my husband does. Marcy introduced me to Gary; and I introduced Annlyn to her husband, Michael; and Annlyn introduced Marcy to hers. But unless the spouses are part of the fireworks business, then it's difficult for them to understand how consuming it is."

She goes on to explain, "Setting up a show, in itself, requires an extraordinary amount of work, which means we're on the road or on the phone handling the whole scheme of things. There are many new and extraneous regulations we're required to follow, which in many ways is good because it keeps the industry safe, and Zambelli Internationale sits on, and supports, the various boards in the industry. There's also quality control to do, as well as all the promotional work. With our involvement with charities, we take on an even greater workload. We donate both our products and our time to worthy causes like the Special Olympics and the Children's Hospital of Pittsburgh. So that requires our attention and time, just as much as the business aspects do—the customer relations, the technical aspects of the work, and the seminars we give. So if one isn't involved in the pyrotechnics industry, he or she just doesn't have a grasp of how overwhelming it is."

Yet, Danabeth, like the rest of her family, wouldn't forgo it for a minute. "My dad," she says, "would go to every single show if he could. His whole face lights up when he watches fireworks; his whole being glows with his love for it. And he knows everything that goes on in the business. It's not unusual to find him leaving the comfort of his office at headquarters to walk the grounds at the plant—visiting his staff, entering the magazines, appearing out of place in his suit and tie while yet looking every bit the man who made it all happen. To love fireworks, fireworks has to be in your blood."

The love of pyrotechnics is practically genetic in the Zambelli family. Their faces radiate when they see sparks and streaks, or hear pops and booms, whether it's for an outside show or an indoor display.

And today, indoor and close-proximity displays are becoming as prevalent as outdoor shows.

"We've been doing 'indoor' for over a decade now, and every year it becomes more popular. Although there are some limitations, there are more advantages."

Zambelli Internationale—experts at indoor pyrotechnics presentations—manages to combine a slew of special effects with the actual explosions. They work off a "cold spark" setup, and use air bursts, confetti, lavish productions and special equipment to make it happen. Danabeth explains that this type of show is great for conventions and other indoor events, and that the nice thing about it is that it takes only a minimum of 15 to 25 feet of clearance.

"We're doing more indoor performances now because clients can see the benefits of not having to worry about the weather and not having to wait until dark to display. Indoor presentations also allow the audience to remain together in a smaller area rather than be scattered all over the grounds as in an outdoor show. Inside, we can do anything—from simple but intriguing exhibits to major, mind-boggling theatrics. We have the technology, experience, equipment, manpower, and creativity to perform dynamic indoor shows of quality comparable to any of our outdoor ones."

*Danabeth (left) and husband Gary Trasatti (right) met on a blind date. Gary owns Pompano Beach-based Florida Textiles. Shown with George and Connie (center). Danabeth and Gary reside in South Florida, where she runs the Boca Raton office with her sister Marcy.*

*Danabeth gives her father a hug after the celebratory fireworks show for the 1997 World Champions Florida Marlins.*

Keeping current, along with being on the leading edge in "pyrotechnica," has made Zambelli Fireworks the undisputed pace setters in the business. Danabeth explains that her company often is on the forefront in creating new colors, inventing computer programs and other electronic wizardry, and displaying from unusual positions, such as on the roof of the U.S. Steel Building, which put the corporation into the *Guiness Book of World Records*.

"The one thing we are trying to improve is our signature shell. We've been experimenting with making a shell that will display Z's, but if it doesn't explode correctly during a show, it looks like N's instead." She grins at the thought.

What does Danabeth consider the most interesting display Zambelli Internationale has ever done?

She shrugs, trying to sort mentally through the thousands her family has put on. "That's tough to answer since we've done so many, but, for me, the Desert Storm show was most dramatic because of the shells we used, the music, and all the yellow ribbons." Desert Storm was a show put on in Washington in 1991 as part of a victory celebration upon the return of U.S. troops from the Persian Gulf after the brief war there forced Iraq to withdraw after invading Kuwait. It is this type of show, to mention only one example, that separates Zambelli Internationale from other pyrotechnics companies. As long as the company keeps on forging ahead, the world will be a happier and brighter place to live.

Danabeth considers what the future holds for the Great Zambellis, the First Family of Fireworks: "We'll keep on going, providing fun and amusement to others. God forbid that anything happens to my father, but I know for a fact that the legacy he will have left us will remain intact simply because he loved the business and we loved him. My brother and sisters and I were raised on electrifying the heavens, and it's all that we really care about. Our goal is to keep our company in the vanguard and bring joy to others. I know I'll always remain in the business in some capacity, and I know the rest of my family will, too, because we care so much about it and about what my parents have built up over the last three decades."

If her father remains in the company when he's pushing a hundred, what will she do? "Love him." She grins, looking at her sister through the glass window between their offices.

# SEVEN

# History of Fireworks

T HE PROVERB "Where there's smoke, there's fire," holds true for fireworks—a pastime relished by old and young. There's something special about shooting colored fire across a black background, something that touches each of us deep inside, brings out the child in us, makes us feel good about being alive. But though fire has been around almost since man's emergence, fireworks have not; instead, they were invented as a byproduct of gunpowder.

The true beginnings of fireworks are unknown, though most experts speculate they originated in the Orient, probably in China. Records indicate that the Chinese ground sulfur and charcoal finely onto paper or placed the grains in a bamboo tube stopped up at one end, and then attached a fuse to the side of the tube and ignited it: *Voila*, the first firecracker. By the 600s, the Chinese had used this gadget in parades and festivals. Around the 10th century, the process of separating potassium nitrate (saltpeter) from

*Fireworks exploding from a palm-tree display on a platform outside the French royal palace as a crowd looks on.*

carbonate was achieved, allowing the Chinese to produce projectiles with gunpowder. In 1130, one of the first fire lances was made. Pyrotechnics historian and specialist Alan St. Brock surmised that a Chinese cook accidentally mixed together powders found at a campsite: perhaps sulfur from fire, charcoal from charred wood, and saltpeter as a salt substitute. When blended, the three ingredients formed the recipe for gunpowder. This gave birth to fireworks and to firecrackers attached to arrows or guns or inserted into cannonballs.

By 1242, England's Friar Roger Bacon had written the first instructions for black powder[1] (the original gunpowder), which is of critical use in fireworks because it determines the power (potency) of the burst, the speed (velocity) the shell will achieve, and the height (aerial altitude) it will reach. Supposedly, Bacon wrote about gunpowder in secret code because of its dangers and its use as a weapon against witchcraft. In the thirteenth century, another monk—a German Franciscan—while trying to invent what is believed to have been gold paint, presumably concocted the $KNO_3$ formula that ushered in gunpowder. Credit, though, must go to the

Chinese, who used gunpowder in weapons against enemies. Seeing that the Chinese could explode the skies with stopped-up bamboo tubes, Marco Polo, who picked up this invention in the late 13th century on a visit to the court of Kublai Kahn, took it back with him to Italy, which began the legacy of the craft.

In the meantime, the Orient was using black powder for ceremonies, and there it was later adapted for military use as a propellant in muskets, cannons, bamboo guns, and other types of weapons. Gunpowder became so popular and crucial that armies had begun taking on men who specialized in its use. But because it was dangerous to mix the formula in one place and transport it to another by mule or similar means, these military explosives specialists ended up blending the formula directly on battlefields. This, of course, did nothing for the popularity of these specialists, who cooked up the highly volatile explosives under the direst conditions, where firing guns and cannons put them and others in jeopardy. Gunpowder's growing popularity resulted in the establishment of small powder-mills all over Europe.

By the 1400s, gunpowder—as the key factor in fireworks—had found its way into nearly every major occasion, from fighting battles to celebrating holidays, weddings and births. In 1487 fireworks were ushered in for coronations; then, again, in the 1500s for welcoming dignitaries from Spain and Portugal on the occasion of a visit to China. By 1532 Charles V, Holy Roman Emperor and king of Spain, was conducting dramatic displays for his religious and royal celebrations. Though the Chinese are credited with bringing about the use of gunpowder, attribution goes to the Italians for transforming fireworks into a high art form during the Renaissance. They shot pyrotechnics into the air,

from the ground, barges, rivers, floats, and fountains. Too, they made use of "green men," adult males with soot spattered on their faces, wearing hats with green leaves cockeyed on their heads, leading parades at fireworks displays. Later, at night, they would scurry behind the scenes, shooting off rockets and shells; their manner of dress camouflaged them among the fireworks.

The early 1600s saw an increasing interest in fireworks, along with a more scientific view of them. A full-scale celebration took place in 1613 in honor of the marriage of James I of England's daughter, Elizabeth, to the Prince Palatine. An even more elaborate display occurred in 1660 when Louis XIV (king of France 1643–1715) emerged with his bride, Marie Theresa; then again, "a year later the birth of the Dauphin was similarly celebrated in several cities of France."[2]

Louis XIV—who was enamored of fireworks— went so far as to build the palace of Versailles for the major purpose of displaying fireworks, during a time when he was trying to economize by selling off his own possessions to help subsidize his military.

One night in 1661 Louis XIV was invited to a gala held by his finance minister, Nicolas Fouquet. The minister hosted a party (supported by government money) for more than 6000 guests, where he executed a magnificent repast, gave away expensive gifts (tiaras, horses), and then concluded the night with ballet dancers, theatrics, and, lastly, fireworks. The pyrotechnics, under the direction of a man named Vigarini, were Louis' favorite, but in the end Fouquet was tossed into jail for abuse of public monies. Then, in 1664, Louis XIV held a festival for 600 people by erupting an entire island in fireworks for five nights straight. At one point in history, even time was proclaimed by a blast of pyrotechnics in the city of Versailles.[3] Less than 100 years later another great fête ensued in honor of the peace treaty at Aix-la-Chappelle that ended the War of the Austrian Succession in 1749. James II (king of England 1685–1701) was so pleased with his staff's pyrotechnic abilities that he knighted his firemaster.

From 1690 to 1712 pyrotechnic displays went on hiatus, but when they did reappear, they did so with gusto, as seen in the peace celebration hosted by Russia's czar (1682–1725), Peter the Great, who sponsored a five-hour display when his son Alexis was born. In fact, Peter himself was somewhat of a pyrotechnician, since he experimented with exploding fireworks and designing show pieces.[4] He's recognized for initiating the popular tradition of shooting fireworks to bring in the New Year.

The 1700s brought about the release of pyrotechnics from the authority of the military and put it into the hands of individuals and commercial establishments. This was seen in 1777 when across America the first Independence Day was celebrated, replete with tons of fireworks. About ten years later, chemist Claude-Louis Berthollet discovered the chlorates that gave pyrotechnics a whole new look.

The power of gunpowder as an explosive in fireworks and weapons prompted the emergence of powdermills throughout Europe. One of those mills was that of Éleuthère Irénée du Pont, who was well-informed in all aspects of explosives, and thus opened a mill in spite of protestations by family members. Eventually settling in America, quiet Irénée set up his company in a lightly populated area because of the potential for fire; yet he wanted the place to be settled enough to allow for transportation and repairs on his equipment. And he needed a

*Fireworks on the Pont-Neuf, in Paris, 1745.*

site that was situated near a rapidly moving stream for a source of power. He found the site on the Brandywine, near Wilmington, Delaware. He constructed the buildings in his yards—called Eleutherian Mills—in the shape of trapezoids, which helped to prevent explosions. Still, accidents happened, averaging one every 14 months. Death at Eleutherian Mills was euphemistically described as "going across the creek."

Three major fires broke out. The first one was in 1817 and killed Irénée's father after he had toiled in the bucket brigade to squelch the fire. Then, a year later, in 1818, a blast, dubbed "the Great Explosion," leveled the mills, killing more than 40 people. And in 1847, Irénée's youngest child, Alexis, died from burns received during an attempt to prevent an explosion. Through the years, E.I. du Pont de Nemours flourished with the help of the U.S. government's purchase of gunpowder to fight the War of 1812 (between the U.S. and England, 1812–1815). Other battles, such as the Mexican War (1846–1848), the Civil War (1861–1865), and later, World Wars I (1914–1918) and II (1939–1945), helped propagate the du Pont company, as did the need for gunpowder for blowing up tree trunks and rocks in settling the Wild West; blasting for gold; killing bears; exploding ditches for construction of the Ohio–Mississippi Canal; blazing right-of-way passages for the railroads; and the U.S. cavalry's handling of disputes between Native Americans and Western settlers.

Years later, under Henry du Pont's leadership

*A night view of the Royal Fireworks in Green Park, St. James, on April 27, 1749.*
Corbis-Bettmann

during the Industrial Revolution, production of gunpowder was greatly increased and the company prospered; private firms began buying gunpowder, which led to the production of blasting powder and dynamite. Soon, pyrotechnics expanded all over the globe, becoming a traditional finale for major events, including the Jubilee of George III (king of England 1760–1820), the 1830 coronation of William IV (king of England 1830–1837), and the 1881 crowning of Russia's Czar Alexander II (which correlated music to fireworks), and the celebration of the end of the Crimean War (1853–1856).

So fireworks gained significant popularity by the 1800s, so much so that rules for their use had to be imposed to reduce the number of accidents. Just as their frequency spiraled, so did methods of display. But none could compare with the Italians when it came to creating ways to put on a dynamic show. For example, in 1892, a 400th anniversary celebration of Columbus' discovery of America was illuminated by fireworks over New York's Brooklyn Bridge.

## Pyrotechnia a l' Italia

Italians as a whole were, and still are, cavalier in their use of pyrotechnics. They're credited with inventing the various colors of fireworks. Ruggieri was one of the pioneers of the business. Although his roots were in Bologna, he settled in France, where he passed his skill down to his descendants, who still practice pyrotechnics today. In fact, nearly all the famous fireworks companies worldwide, and particularly in the United States, are family-owned by people of Italian descent.

Back in the 18th and 19th centuries, Italian pyrotechnicians relied on the use of what was referred to as "the machine" or "the temple" since elaborate set pieces were not yet in vogue. These machines were huge structures with grand doorways and windows, detailed figurines and paintings, adorned with gingerbread molding and domed turrets, enhanced by grandiose staircases showcasing finely crafted newels and spindles. The machines opened and released the fireworks. In themselves, they were a sight to observe, prompting many spectators to attend fireworks shows just to behold the machines. Even famed painters of the time got involved in pyrotechnics by helping to design displays. A major reason the actual fireworks show was anticlimactic compared with the machines was that fireworks colors at the time were only yellow or amber from sulfur, with perhaps a hint of green from zinc. Since most fireworks colors had yet to be invented, fireworks didn't draw the crowds they do today. Thus, the machines were more popular than

the actual pyrotechnic displays. Over time, these set pieces were embellished with actors, props, theatrical scenes, and transparencies.

Since their inception, fireworks have been considered symbolic of life itself, with messages of love, romance, special events (victories, coronations, weddings, even funerals), and the like written across the tablet of the sky for all to see. Shows were, and are, designed to be theatrical productions with such built-in meanings. Soon, other countries besides Italy were reveling in fireworks, with each country manufacturing shells characteristic of its own nation. Italy held supreme, especially for its salutes (booms), but Americans gained fame for their continuous multibreak shells, while France was noted for the sharpness of color in its displays. In Canada, willows with long sprays took prominence, while stars that darted on explosion gave Brazil distinction. Asia preferred stars arrayed in chrysanthemum formations; China and Japan took first place. By the 1840s the chemical potassium chlorate was discovered and used in pyrotechnics to expand the color range and sharpen the hues. From the inception of fireworks until now, it took hundreds of years before the color blue could be detonated—the most difficult color to make—though purple is challenging, too, since it's the newest color.

The ingredients of fireworks are formulated into "recipes" that are highly guarded by the owners of pyrotechnics companies, and usually written in black books that remain in the possession of the family patriarch. Generally, no backup copies exist, and in many cases, nothing is written at all, but rather remains in the memory of the patriarch, who shares the recipes at the appropriate time with the heir to the business. These trade secrets are passed from generation to generation in an oral tradition so as not to risk losing the cookbook and having it fall

into the wrong hands. It is a fact that in America nearly all the recipes are written in Italian or were derived from that language.

Today the basis of those recipes remains the same. What has changed is the technology. Computerization and lasers have had a major effect on fireworks. Now shows are digitally generated, and shells are fired electrically allowing for phenomenal visual and sound effects, as well as for improved safety practices. Music is choreographed to the pieces, which may be aerial displays, set designs, or a combination of both—all of which makes spectators want more and hope the presentation never ends. In our current high-tech world, nearly any type of fireworks show is possible. You can have pyrotechnics shot from the highest building in the world, waterfalls tumbling with fireworks, peonies hurled from barges where water doubles the vision, fire so vibrantly pigmented in multibreak shells that you're left panting—all through the miracle of computerization.

Displays today can be fired manually, electronically, or on site at the firing field from Windows-based laptop computers, which send signals via the Marti System with SMPTE codes. This is all synchronized to music and special effects to give a spectacular dance recital replete with ballet pliés, pirouettes, color, thunder, and—of course—applause and bravos from jubilant crowds. This, however, sounds simpler than it is. Choreographed fireworks shows require work, time, and technical skill that, when calibrated in unison, yield a presentation that leaves bystanders in awe. Naturally, the bigger and more lavish the display, the greater the amount of work and time it takes to coordinate sound engineering to pyrotechnic detonations.

Zambelli Internationale is a worldwide pioneer

*The castle and bridge of St. Angelo, Rome, with a grand display of fireworks from the summit of the castle.* Corbis-Bettmann

in technologically matching music and choreography to raging pyrotechnics, giving its displays a flourish and flare unequalled anywhere. So with computerized advancements at the fireworkers' fingertips, any pyrotechnics show can metamorphose into a major Broadway production.

We've come a long way since the Chinese invented fireworks. Who knows what else this industry might create to overwhelm its audiences?

# EIGHT

# Firing Display, and Manufacturing Fireworks

To WATCH A FIREWORKS SHOW, you would never believe how much work goes into it. And the show seems to be over almost as soon as it starts. The average cost of a 20-minute electronically fired show runs about $40,000.[5] To the uninitiated, that seems like a lot of money for so little display time, but after you learn what goes into a theatrical fireworks display, the $40,000 will seem like a smidgen for a whole lot of work. Following, then, is what's entailed in a typical presentation.

## Manufacturing

If you merely look at a shell, it seems like an easy product to make, but in reality there's much that goes into the manufacturing of fireworks. Inside that volatile object is energy ready to burst open, much the same way an unvented pressure cooker erupts violently when heated.

The two types of aerial shells—cylindrical and spherical—commonly run in sizes such as 3", 4", 5", 6", 8", 12", 16", and 24", though even larger shells, such as five-footers (in length), have been created for special occasions. Sixteen-inch shells are generally the largest used in a show; rarely are 24" ones shot, but there have been instances when gigantic shells have been created and fired. A shell is measured by its diameter, not by its circumference. Fireworks can be shot into the air (aerial shells), displayed at low level, or fired from ground level—or a combination of all of these.

*Aerial shells* are slid snugly into mortars, where they're propelled by a lift charge to burst high in the air at 200 to 1200 feet. A shell's height of ascent is proportional to its size.[6] *Low-level* shells display up to 100 to 150 feet in the air and burst from the ground up, rather than from the sky down.[7] In this case, fireworks such as mines, barrages of Roman candles, and "cakes" are set off into the sky from the ground, whereas *ground-level* fireworks remain on the ground, as seen in gerbs, or lances inserted into set pieces, fountains, wheels, girandolas, colored fire, waterfalls, and so on. *Indoor fireworks*, which may be considered a fourth type, are really a combination of the latter two and are becoming more popular. Specifically, indoor fireworks use gerbs, fountains, waterfalls, colored fire, concussions, sparkle pots, flash pots, and air bursts.

While the way fireworks are shot is important

*The difference between one fireworks company's display and another's is the "recipe." George Zambelli, Sr., says, "My competitors would love to get their hands on my black book."*

to the display, of equal significance is how they're composed. Essentially, only 30 chemicals make up the basic ingredients of all fireworks. Which chemicals are used is determined by the availability of the ingredients, their cost, and their degree of stability and compatibility. The secret is in the strategic packing of each shell (the arrangement and mix of pellet types or stars) and the placement of fuses. Chlorine added to metallic salts intensifies color; thus, how finely ground the powder is, the type of binder used, and the order in which the chemicals are mixed control the vibrancy of hues in a fireworks show. So what's procurable by the fireworker and how he packs each shell becomes critical to a display. The difference between one fireworks company's display and another's is the "recipe." George Zambelli, Sr., says, "My competitors would love to get their hands on my black book." But no matter what the ingredients, flash powder produces the sound (the "boom") of fireworks while black powder serves as the propellant and the "igniter" of the time fuse.

At Zambelli Internationale, all fireworks are still made by hand, to avoid sparks or static electricity generated by machinery. Of course, smoking is banned, as is hair combing, and workers must hit a copper plate before entering manufacturing bunkers, to discharge any sparks. Light bulbs are specially encased in wire mesh, and floors are lined with sawdust. Here's an overview of how aerial fireworks are manufactured:

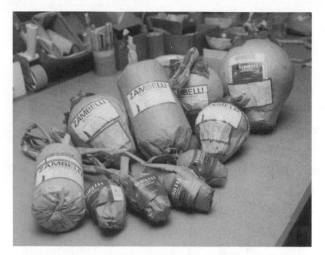

1. *Finished spherical and cylindrical shells.*

2. *A sieve filters and sifts the chemicals, formulated to create explosive and combustible materials.*

3. *In the cutting room, a pyrotechnician pounds and kneads the dampened chemicals into the shape of a loaf of bread.*

4. *A master craftsman dices the loaf into stars, which exhibit as colors in the dark sky.*

**1.** An integral part of a spherical or cylindrical shell's structure is its casing, whether it's a single break or multibreak shell. The *casing* gives a shell its form and ability to withstand high internal pressure. These casings are made of heavy paper, cardboard, or plastic, with the thickness determining the force needed to burst open.

Each shell casing is filled with several ounces of explosive and combustible materials that provide color and special effects. The *stars* create the color;

*1. A pyrotechnician checking the stars' degree of dryness.*

*2. Stars are placed in casings around the bursting charge.*

*3. A highly skilled technician inspects a shell in the making and its protruding time fuse.*

the *flash powder* yields flashes of light and resounding noise; and the *components* give unique and peculiar sounds and animation.

**2.** In the "cutting room," a pyrotechnician mixes the chemicals with water to bind them together before pounding them into the form of a loaf of bread. This loaf is diced into shapes of stars or cubes and then dusted with gunpowder to help ignition. On sunny days the mixture is set outside to dry, while in inclement weather it's dried in "drying rooms" by heaters. Special effects are produced by hand-loading or press-loading small cylindrical components. Holes are bored into the sides in various directions to change their animation, sound, and visual effects.

**3.** The stars or components are placed in the casings around the *bursting charge*, which is the explosive powder that will not only ignite the internal effects but, in the case of low combustible stars, will cause the shells to burst open. The balance between the amount of bursting charge and the strength of the wall of the shell will determine the shape and width of the shell's visual display.

The bursting charge can be inserted inside the shell in a preloaded flash bag attached to the time fuse, or the stars or components can be loaded around a hollow paper tube, filling the container. It might take as many as a thousand stars to fill one large break. When filling the container with stars or components, it's important not to create any friction. The gunpowder—which serves as the ignition and the casing's bursting charge—is poured into the hollow tube to settle into the center of the casing; then the paper tube is removed.

**4.** A *time delay fuse* is then placed in the lid of the casing. The length of this fuse will determine the break time (the amount of time the shell will travel in the air after ignition before it bursts open). The

1. *A technician is spiking a canister with heavy string in the spiking room.*

2. *In the pasting room, star-filled breaks are wrapped in damp pasty paper before being returned to the spiking room.*

3. *Casings are set outside in nice weather to dry until they harden. In inclement weather, they are dried inside.*

4. *A spiked shell (canister with string wrapped around it) is examined before being passed back to the pasting room. The process of going back and forth between pasting and spiking rooms is a repetitive one.*

length and placement of fuses are important because they determine the timing and quality of explosions.

**5.** Each casing is taken to the "spiking room," where heavy string is wrapped around it several times to form a web and grid pattern. Now referred to as a *canister* it is taken to a "pasting room," where the star-filled breaks are wrapped in damp pasty brown paper, much like papier-mâché, and dried until hardened. Next, the canister is passed back to the spiking room and again to the pasting room to give each shell the outside-wall strength needed for maximum display quality.

**6.** Multibreak shells are built utilizing multiple casings or compartments stacked on top of each other. Variation of the time-fuse lengths causes them to break in the air in sequence or timed precision, consecutively, to give a progression of color effects and/or sounds. Zambelli is the leader in traditional multibreak shells.

**7.** After the internal display quality of the aerial shell has been constructed, a side fuse is connected to the canister. The *side fuse* which will instantaneously ignite the lift charge and propel the shell into the air, is attached in the "finishing room," where the break shells are rolled in a dry, brown, glued kraft paper. The kraft paper is approximately eight inches longer than the overall length of the canister. This provides a space at the bottom of the shell to house the *black lift powder*, which is an explosive or bursting powder composed of saltpeter (or potassium nitrate), charcoal, and sulfur. Its volatility makes it dangerous; thus, a spark can be easily ignited. The precise number of ounces of black lift powder is determined by the size and weight of each aerial shell, so that an individual shell can reach its designated height (trajectory) before the bursting charge is ignited by the time fuse.

Pyrotechnic string-tie is utilized to seal the bottom of the kraft paper that houses the black lift

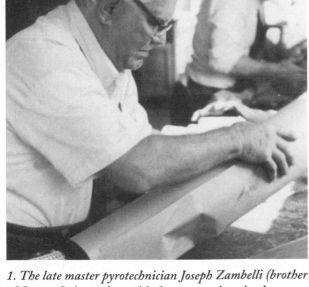

1. *The late master pyrotechnician Joseph Zambelli (brother of George Sr.) attaches a side fuse to a canister in the finishing room.*

2. *Joseph Zambelli inserts a leader into the kraft paper at the top of the shell and secures it with pyrotechnic string-tie to finish the manufacture of the shell.*

powder. The excess kraft paper is severed with a lift sharp knife. A *leader* (black match fuse), which ultimately will extend outside the firing mortar, is then inserted into the top of the kraft paper that stretches beyond the canister. The top of the craft paper is then tied with pyrotechnic string to complete the shell. This craft paper also protects the aerial shell so that it can be boxed and transported to a show where "setup" will take place.

**8.** A random selection of each type of aerial shell is removed from its manufacturing lot and test-fired at a designated site on the plant's premises to ascertain the quality, safety, and efficiency of the shells. Tests are often performed several times a day.

Although the manufacture of aerial shells is the most complex operation, the production and processing of all pyrotechnic devices and procedures require painstaking and meticulous one-on-one hand-crafting. In addition to the different workshops where shells are made, other workstations are used for constructing set or ground pieces, such as the "design and paper cutting" area, the "carpentry room," and the "lances room."

# Setting Up an Electronically Fired Show

At the display site, the Zambelli crew arrives to position mortars for firing. The crew works from a schematic, which is a design of how the show should be set up for electronic firing. Racks and "mortar boxes" are stationed. *Mortars* are long tubes made of cardboard, fiberglass, plastic, or metal, from which the shells are launched. Shells and their corresponding mortars are numbered based on a script that correlates the firing sequence. Shells must be placed into the proper mortars in order for pressure

to build and catapult them into the air. Hence, the diameter of the shell must match the diameter of the mortar. After the shell is lowered into the mortar, a *squib* (often referred to as an *electrical match*) is inserted into the leader. The electrical match is then bridged to the firing slat so that an electrical current will charge through the wires to ignite the shell when an operator flips a switch at the firing panel or control box via a laptop computer.

**1.** Shells are lowered into their corresponding mortar.

**2.** The leader of each shell is hung over the side of the mortar.

**3.** The leader of each shell is connected to an electrical match (squib).

**4.** The electric match is fastened to the slat (web), which, in turn, is coupled to the lines and cables, and to the firing panel or computer (when the electrical match receives its electrical impulse, it will ignite the leader, which will simultaneously ignite the lift charge and the time fuse).

**5.** The lit leader kindles the lift charge at the bottom of the shell. The black lift powder rages, thrusting the shell out of the mortar and into the sky.

**6.** The hurtled shell reaches apogee, at which point the time fuse ignites the bursting charge, and the shell explodes. The shell's contents break in proper sequence to give an array of colors (usually two, but more are possible) and a cannonade of sounds. A Rainbow Comet spews eight colors—the most from any single shell.

Not all fireworks shows use only aerial shells. Some are a combination of ground pieces, and low-level effects, and aerial shells. So, then, in addition to setting up shells and their racks or mortar boxes, the crew must also assemble the set or stationary pieces. Sometimes scaffolding must be erected to do this, particularly for the large wooden sets.

When a performance is completed, clean-up begins, starting with the hunt for nonfired shells, although nonfiring rarely occurs. In the meantime, the crew continues to "tear down", pulling mortars out of the ground, collecting and discarding casings, and disassembling set pieces. The crew must still pack their gear and eat dinner in the face of having to be at another site the following day. During the Fourth of July, Zambelli has hundreds of crews on the road, each doing many shows in a short period of time.

Zambelli conducts a postshow evaluation as well, so firing the shells isn't the end of any presentation. In many respects, it's only the middle.

## Types of Fireworks

Although most fireworks have the same basic composition, many other factors—determining luster, intensity, quality, and tenor, as well as the tone of their salutes—go into their manufacture. Secret recipes, containing chemical compositions and directions and techniques for grinding, mixing, and packing the powders, enhance the basic ingredients to creates the "oomph," so that the colors of one fireworks company may be better than those of another. Although new fireworks colors are developed on an ongoing basis and through trial and error, only clusters of elements account for the entire spectrum of fireworks hues, such as strontium carbonate for red; barium chlorate for green; sodium oxalate for yellow; magnesium or aluminum for white; copper for blue; charcoal or iron for orange or amber. Copper chloride manages to overcome the challenge of creating purple. Zambelli Internationale is known for having concocted one of the richest purples ever to paint the

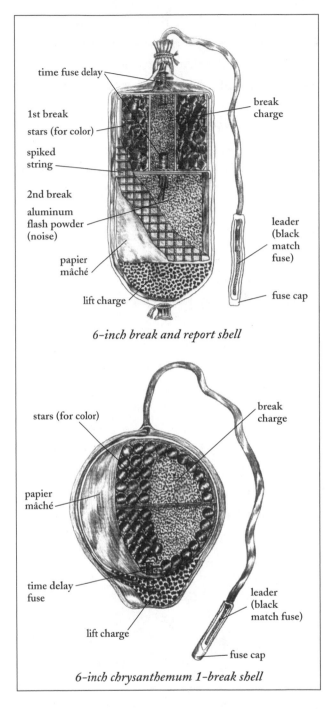

*6-inch break and report shell*

*6-inch chrysanthemum 1-break shell*

heavens. When charcoal is added to the chemicals, the shells yield sparkles and a flittering effect; when parlon is added to colors, it enhances and brightens the visual effects so that red, for example, becomes a brilliant, electric hue.

Here are a few basic types of fireworks:

**1. Bombs, firecrackers, flash crackers:** Tightly packed gunpowder that blows the containers apart.

**2. Cherry Bombs, M-80s, silver salutes:** Powerful, extremely dangerous, and illegal fireworks that are banned in all states. They can contain 40 times as much explosive as permitted by law.

**3. Fountains or gerbs:** Spray-colored sparks emitted from a pyramid-like or cylindrical structure (tube).

**4. Lances:** Thin paper tubes, about 4" to 5" long, filled with multitudes of color-producing chemicals that burn for 55 to 60 seconds.

**5. Niagara Falls sticks:** Thin paper tubes between 8 and 13 inches long, filled with a special chemical composition and primed to ignite. These are hung on a cable approximately 16 inches apart to create a waterfall effect.

**6. Rockets:** Cylindrical devices attached to a long stick for guidance, with a nose cone. Similar to Roman candles, rockets are loaded with a propellant and other types of pyrotechnics materials, such as serpents, whistles, stars, or flash powder.

**7. Roman candles:** Long, cylindrical devices that contain stars packed one atop another, with a layer of powder between stars, creating repetitive, fireball-like projectiles.

**8. Shells:** Cylinders or spheres filled with explosive powders and stars that break in the air to give color and sound.

**9. Smoke bombs:** Containers of chemicals that emit smoke but don't explode.

**10. Snakes:** Chemicals encased in a packet that, when lit, crawl out like a snake. Some states permit these for home use.

**11. Sparklers:** Metal wire coated in a slurry of chemicals to give off a shower of sparks that, when lit, reach temperatures as high as 1,800 degrees. Some states permit this type of firework for home use .

**12. Star mines:** An eruption of stars skyward from the mouth of a cylindrical tube, creating a volcanic effect.

**13. Strobes:** Small canisters approximately 1½" by 2" filled with strobing composition (white, red, purple, green, etc.), which bubble and strobe when ignited.

**14. Wheels:** Colored pots affixed to the circumference of a wheel's wooden rim, creating a colorful effect. Rockets or drivers are obliquely attached to the radial of the wheel to allow it to spin. Pinwheels are a common form of this firework.

To complicate matters, each of these shell bursts can be choreographed to music or a laser show, or a combination of both, as well as other special effects. Synchronizing all of this takes time, talent, and experience. Zambelli Fireworks was a pioneer in presenting high-tech musicals in the sky.

The number and type of explosives allowed in one's possession are dictated by state and federal rules, with nearly all states prohibiting the use of fireworks by individuals.

So enjoy the fireworks but leave the shooting of pyrotechnics to the experts.

*Master pyrotechnicians: left, the late Joe Zambelli, the eldest brother, and right, Lou Zambelli, the youngest brother, with special Italian multibreak shells.*

# NINE

# Behind the Scenes at the Manufacturing Plants

WHEN DRIVING ON THE OUTSKIRTS of New Castle, look closely enough and beyond the wide girths of oaks, maples, and Douglas firs, and you might glimpse little shacks dotting the banks and slopes. These small structures are the hallmarks of the Zambellis' livelihood, as they're the bunkers for making fireworks.

Zambelli has two major plants: Nashua Harbor and English Avenue. The former is where all the fireworks are made today, while much of the latter—the original plant—was razed by an explosion in October 1997. When the old plant, after more than 100 years in existence, went up in smoke, luckily no one was injured, but nearly the entire operation was destroyed. So the Nashua Harbor plant is now the main factory for fireworks production and manufacturing. The gated entrance opens to a spread of more than 1,000 acres, of which several plants lie visible to the naked eye,

*The Zambelli plant in the New Castle countryside covers at least 780 developed acres and has more than 100 manufacturing areas and storage blockhouses, a dock, shipping facilities, magazines, and offices. Some structures are built into the rolling hillsides.*

shipping stations, and one plant office. These buildings with their snaking walkways seem to flow with the roll of the hills, and thus, from a distance, appear to wind around and up and down mounds of earth. Some of the magazines are as old as the plant's 40-plus years, but all bunkers containing explosives are made of concrete, and each concrete shed is protected by a cinder-block wall for containing any flare-ups. Facilities not constructed of concrete are limited to workstations, storage, and offices. One can scan slopes of concrete boxes dotting terra firma, knowing more land lies beyond what vision allows. "A new bunker is being completed and will be one-of-a-kind in the fireworks industry because of its construction and capabilities. It's 64 feet wide and 200 feet long, and will handle 10 trucks being loaded with mortars at one time. All the racks and mortars will be held in

while the view of the rest must be fleshed out by walking deep into the woods. Seven hundred and eighty acres are developed, housing more than 100 structures; 320 acres are yet to be cultivated. But at the rate the company is growing, the remaining acreage will soon be unfolded, too. Plant office worker Wayne Moser says, "We're building two to three magazines every year. Our biggest jump happened between 1980 and 1984, when the company underwent much construction, such as the building of the dock, shipping facilities, and several magazines. It's been uphill ever since."

Of the 100 structures, only 82 buildings are discernible to the eye, since many are built into the hillsides. The original 48 are visibly numbered. Every building is designated a specific security level and is accessible only to those authorized. The buildings comprise workstations, mixing and press rooms, storage bunkers, magazines, fabrication and

*Magazines containing explosives are constructed of concrete and cinder block. A cinder block wall serves as a buffer between magazines. Great care is taken with security and safety at the plant.*

one place in the building; and there will be an office and an electrical room to store the equipment for electronically firing fireworks. It's a pyrotechnician's dream," inserts Marcy Zambelli.

On a wintry day, blowing snow and gales pick up, making Wayne Moser tuck his head inside his coat collar as he says, "We're not sure what destroyed the English Avenue plant, but a spark detonated the bunker and everything blew. We're just glad no one was hurt. As George always says, 'Things can be replaced; people can't.'"

Wayne has worked for Zambelli Fireworks for more than a dozen years, and he's only one of many with a long employment history with the company. He explains, "Some staff have worked here for decades. [Mr. Zambelli] and his family are good people."

These "good people" gear up for New Year's fireworks celebrations and Independence Day right after Thanksgiving, when 33 plant employees swell to 50, then to 70, to produce "Thunder Over Louisville," and finally to thousands for the Fourth of July, not counting those working at headquarters or branch offices, or the reps stationed worldwide. Wayne comments, "We're a big operation, the largest fireworks company in the world. We're proud of the quality of the work we do and the excellent safety record we've achieved and maintained."

With wind battering his face, Wayne walks the paved, graveled, and earthen paths to the plant office, where heat fills the brightly lit, computerized facility. It houses small offices for transportation management, accounting, inventory, training, and other departments. On the way he chats with plant manager Howard (Howie) Simmons, who's worked for Zambelli since the 1960s. Pressed for time, Wayne turns the tour over to Simmons, who walks into the office of transportation.

## Transportation

Entering the office of training, testing, and transportation is akin to stepping into a room of sunshine, where blinking lights animate a bank of computers and high-tech equipment. This office handles itinerary and shooting operations, but the transportation of explosives is a primary function. It focuses on the adherence to regulations concerning the conveyance of explosives from the plant to display sites, and the licensing of individuals involved in transporting and shooting. Ronald Wethli and Ron Snyder oversee this area, which entails about 200 drivers and 1,200 shooters. Says Wethli, "Shooters must be trained, licensed, and experienced, and have their pyrotechnician's license and CDL (commercial driver's license), which requires hazardous-materials training and the passing of necessary tests."

Wethli keeps track of shipping files and all the drivers' and shooters' records. Via a special computer program, he can map out a driver's route from corporate headquarters to the first display site, and from there to the next, and so on. Occasionally Wethli will also check with state troopers to verify safe routing on some roads. Drivers must explicitly follow the route chartered by Wethli and must keep logs of their transport programs. No deviation from the computerized route is permitted unless drivers first check with Ron. This is because there are transportation rules that prohibit drivers of explosive materials from ferrying such loads over certain routes. Tunnels, populated areas, and some bridges are off-limits.

"If we find out a violation has been committed by a driver, he's terminated by the company, fined excessively, and may face various legal charges," says Ron Wethli, who walks out of his office to the entry area of the building, where he posts a sign informing employees of training classes, then returns to his office to track his truckdrivers. The staff in this office frequently give seminars to Zambelli employees located in various regions of the country to educate and update them on safety and routing specifications.

## Inventory

L eaving the transportation office, Simmons unbuttons his winter coat as he moves to the office of John Gallick, who's in charge of inventory and compliance with rules on storehousing of explosives. Says Gallick, "The BATF [Bureau of Alcohol, Tobacco, and Firearms] regulates us, and requires that we keep a daily balance of each gram of explosive, and know where every gram is. They do spotchecks and annual inspections and review our logs. How much explosive a facility can store or work with is based on factors such as the type of storage structure, the distance between buildings, the kinds of magazines, and the amount of manufacturing done." Gallick looks thoughtful before continuing. "You know, some people are under the mistaken impression that it's no big deal to possess explosive materials, like gunpowder. But no one can just open a fireworks company. The handling of explosives is

*"The handling of explosives is serious business, and anyone who possesses hazardous materials is responsible to the government," explains John Gallick, who handles inventory and storehousing compliance for the company; shown here with Marcy (left) and Danabeth (right) Zambelli.*

serious business, especially since 9/11, and anyone who possesses hazardous materials is responsible to the government." Gallick performs regular plant inventory checks, and if something is out of balance—say, explosives are missing—he immediately contacts the state police and the BATF, as theft of fireworks is a federal offense.

The computer's printer pounds away, sputtering out sheets of listings. Gallick adds, "We're automated at Zambelli Internationale in every phase of work. We have laser guns for inventory marking and routing, and we're computerized for recording our large stock." He scans the printout, mumbling, "We take our work seriously. And wouldn't you want us to?"

## Shells, Shells, Shells

S immons exits from John's office to outside, saying, "It's not unusual for it to snow now." It's early November and the wintry gray sky is reminiscent of a mid-January. He opens the door to a work-station, where Viola Babel stands over a counter laid out with shells. Like all Zambelli plant workers, she's wearing a company shirt and rubber-soled shoes so as not to set off sparks. Overhead, the ceiling light is encased in a glass globe, and the light switch on the wall is contained in a protective casing.

Babel is examining and repackaging shells that were returned from a rained-out performance. "My job is to inspect all shells before they revert to inventory. In the event one is irreparably damaged, it must be disposed of in accordance with the regulations of the Environmental Protection Agency. We have a specific EPA-approved burn unit on site for disposal." Her fingers run over the shells with the adroitness of an executive typist. "What I'm working on here are mostly 8" shells, but they come in various sizes. We manufacture large ones, too."

Simmons nods, interjecting, "Each shell size requires specific distances to shoot and discharge it, based on rules and regulations set by the National Fire Protection Agency [NFPA]. We call this the 'firing zone.' The larger the diameter of the shell, the larger the diameter of the firing zone required;

the bigger the shell, the larger and heavier it is, thus requiring a wider zone. This is paramount and is done to ensure crowd safety."

In the background, Babel, who's been with Zambelli for more than 12 years, is humming a light tune. Simmons adds, "You can't have radios in here, so Viola sings. This room is especially designed to prevent sparks from erupting. It has no open flame, and pipes and electricity run underground." Heated as a "dry room," here shells are placed in winter to dry the papier-mâché.

Babel details the shells in her workstation, explaining that patterned ones unfold in shapes of stars, hearts, smiley faces, yellow ribbons, corporate logos, and a slew of other designs; flag shells emit different types of flags on parachutes.

Simmons interjects, "Flash powder—aluminum and high explosives—goes into salutes, the noise-makers, while 'smokes' are powder mixtures, which come in different sizes and give off colored fogs and mists." He nods to Babel and leaves her bunker, heading for the break room, which is the only place where plant workers are allowed to have a cigarette, because it's isolated and no flammable materials are

*Viola Babel sings as she works, inspecting shells. The room is specially designed to prevent sparks from erupting, so no radios are allowed.*

*Zambelli fireworks shells are made by hand, much as they were hundreds of years ago, with kraft paper, paste, powder and closely guarded secret formulas and designs.*

*The shipping and packing room, where shells are placed in bins. The shells are hand-picked and packed for each display.*

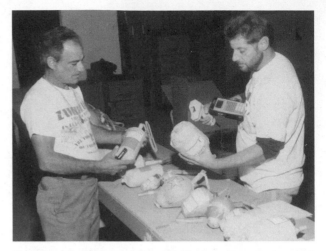

*Raymond Loffredo and Don Wolford use battery-operated inventory guns to pack choreographed programs.*

permitted inside. Howard is momentarily warmed; he turns and ventures back outdoors to the shipping building, which is connected to a series of adjoining magazines housing the various inventory in bins on shelves. Inside are Ray Loffredo and Don Wolford, who between them have traveled the world setting up Zambelli displays and have put in a total of more than 50 years at Zambelli, Inc., with Ray alone having worked almost 37 of them.

In the shipping building Simmons says, "Here is where we pack, load, and ship the shells. Everything's done to a scripted firing sequence. This script is generated by a computer when the choreographer outlines when to fire certain shells to music. The shells are packed in numbered and labeled boxes that correspond to the firing numbers so that setup on the site is more easily achieved." Because Zambelli does thousands of displays a year, each one is assigned a show number. "Our company," says Simmons, "is big enough to buy, store, and pack shells far in advance, allowing us to stockpile for future shows. This gives us a ready supply at all times, which is something most fireworks companies can't do. Another benefit of being large is that

we can set up and perform any show on short notice. The only problem is securing the proper permits in time."

Agreeing, Wolford explains, "Once a show is a go, this is what we do: When we arrive at the show site, we unload the equipment from the truck. The shells' mortars are buried about three-quarters deep into sand-filled mortar boxes and are set up according to the script. Shells are then slid, in numbered order, into their respectively sized mortars. Squibs, which are electrical matches, are inserted into the fuses for electrical firing. Predesigned constructed stationary pieces are erected and anchored into the ground after lances and fuses have first been affixed to the framework. This is all very time-consuming. Everything then gets hooked up to the master control computer. Lastly, we fire the show. Usually a fire-truck is nearby and the fire marshal or his or her representative is at every site, but we always go beyond what's required by law."

"And," adds Simmons, "because of our safety record, we have one of the best insurance ratings. There are lots of regulations to follow, such as those mandated by federal and state policies, as well as

ABOVE: *George Zambelli lights up; a man living his dream.*

LEFT: *A White House visit with President Jimmy Carter. Left to right, Melanie, Danabeth, Connie, George Jr., President Carter with Alison, and George Sr.*

OPPOSITE PAGE: **Nonstop thunder at Thunder Over Louisville, Louisville, Kentucky.**

ABOVE LEFT: **President Ronald Reagan greets George and Connie at the Congressional Picnic on the White House lawn.**

ABOVE RIGHT: **President and Mrs. George Bush at Camp Kennebunkport with George Jr. (left) and George Sr. (right).**

LEFT: **Fireworks magic at the Three Rivers Regatta, Pittsburgh, Pennsylvania, where the Ohio, Monongahela, and Allegheny Rivers meet.**

BELOW: **"Fire and Ice"—fireworks light the sky and snow over the world-famous American Niagara Falls.**

Big Red Tailgate Party, Monday Night Football, Oct. 21, 2002, sponsored by H.J. Heinz Co.

George Sr. and George Jr. do a photo shoot for an article on the Zambelli family business, "Secret Capitals," that appeared in Time magazine.

George W. Bush greets the Zambelli family at a September 5, 2001, dinner honoring the president of Mexico. Left to right, Jared, Alison, Michael Jr., George Jr., President George W. Bush holding his dog Barney, George Sr., and Connie.

*Clemente Bridge Lighting Ceremony, sponsored by Duquesne Light, Pittsburgh, PA.*

*Zambelli Fireworks exhibits many displays in the Caribbean and in Latin America. This fireworks production was exhibited for the Virgin Islands Carnival, St. Thomas, Virgin Islands.*

*One of George Sr.'s most memorable moments, meeting Pope John Paul II in Baltimore, Maryland. Zambelli Fireworks performed a display for the Pope's visit.*

*Brilliant sprays of color splatter the mirrored canvas.*

ABOVE: *Desert Storm Homecoming—National Victory Celebration, Washington, D.C.*

OPPOSITE PAGE: *A dramatic finale above the historical site of Mount Rushmore.* Photo courtesy of South Dakota Tourism

*ABOVE LEFT: A proud celebration for Zambelli Fireworks. 100th birthday of the "Statue of Liberty," July 4, 1986.*

*ABOVE RIGHT: Skies above the Suncoast Casino are lit up Las Vegas-style, celebrating its anniversary.*

*RIGHT: A glorious celebration for the 300th anniversary of Yale University. Zambelli created an electric logo of a "Y" that stood 40 feet wide and 50 feet high and utilized 4,500 feet of blue lights.*

Cardboard, plastic, or fiberglass mortars (firing tubes) are secured in wooden racks and braced before loading with shells and wiring.

Shells can be fired from single tubes made of steel or fiberglass. These are buried in sand or sand mortar boxes for stability.

A pyrotechnician prepares a shell by carefully placing a squib (an electric match) in the fuse of the shell.

Squib wire is attached to a slat. A cable connects the slat to the firing board. The firing board sends the electronic signals to fire, providing split-second timing choreographed to music.

those on the local—city and county—levels. We don't send fireworks to just anyone or any organization wanting to display."

As Simmons speaks, he glances around the packing room, which is lined with cartons of shells ready to be transported to a show. Each box is specially manufactured to meet required standards in labeling, size, strength, and class, as well as in durability as dropped from a particular height.

Explains Loffredo, "These boxes are loaded onto trucks sent out to display sites. On the Fourth, we're so busy that we have to recruit trucks from wherever we can get them, including Budget and Ryder. At times we also ship via air freight and FedEx. Zambelli alone, has 200 trucks." Loffredo smiles as he recalls his broad experience firing shows

*Wayne Moser inspects one of the mortar storage facilities.*

*Computers and inventory software allow a sophisticated inventory-control program where every shell is accounted for at all times.*

*A 24-inch shell is carefully lowered into a giant mortar, buried deep in the sand.*

since he's been with the company: "The company's grown large, fast, because we're the best at what we do. I've been all over the world—Venezuela, Philippines, Saudi Arabia, Guam, China, Europe—and I still like 'Thunder Over Louisville.' We put on one heckuva show there! It takes 30 people and 10 days, along with 15 trailer truckloads of shells and equipment, to assemble that show." Wolford, too, has traveled the globe: "Guam's an interesting show to do, but difficult."

In a room adjacent to the packing area sits an imposing supply of shells that allows for technicians to pull the sizes and types ordered, based on the script. Every time a shell is removed, the laser gun registers it for inventory purposes, so any explosive that gets moved is instantly accounted for.

Outside again, Simmons' rosy cheeks meet with frigid air as he treads the hill towards a large pole building where mortars and racks reach the ceiling, requiring a cherry picker to remove them for loading onto trucks. Mortars range in size and weight, with the largest, heaviest ones lying outside the building because they're too big to store inside. He explains, "Mortars can be made to any size, but they

*Jerry Black works on the lance press, making lances for set pieces.*

60 seconds each. Longer lances are available, but the 4" to 5" ones are most common. They're loaded by hand and can be "colorized" for shows. Lances are placed onto set pieces for igniting a design. Simmons says Jerry makes 144 lances (a gross) about 20 times a day, which comes out to around 2,880 lances manufactured every day to meet Zambelli's demand.

Says Black, "In the design of the one-frame U.S. flag, the frame takes about 40 lances for the blue, 100 for the white, and 100 for the red. And that's just one set piece. You can imagine how many lances we go through around Independence Day when we're doing about 1,800 shows that holiday week. Numerous shows take several set pieces." Jerry pauses to concentrate on sifting the powder, filling the lance tubes, pressing all 144, applying the black powder, and smoothing it.

Simmons looks over Black's shoulder, then leaves the magazine, gently shutting the door behind him. He trudges to a workstation that emits

commonly run a few inches to 16 inches in width, though they've been made 40-some inches, as well as 8 feet tall. The smaller mortars are made of plastic, fiberglass, or cardboard, but the bigger and heavier ones—8, 10, 12, 16, and 24 inches—are composed of metal or steel. Mortars can be contained in racks that can be all the same size or a combination of different sizes. For example, a combo rack holds two 4" shells, two 5" shells, and one 6" shell. But shells have to fit securely into their mortars and yet be free enough to go flying out when fired." Outside the storage structure lie two huge black mortars, 24 inches in diameter—wide enough to hold the same-sized shell. A thin white layer of snow covers them, but their awesome size is easy to discern even from a distance.

Simmons pushes on, entering the magazine of Jerry Black, who's been dubbed "Lancelot" because he makes lots of lances. Lances are rolled, thin, cylindrical papers containing pyrotechnic powder. They are about 4 to 5 inches long, and burn around

*Graphic artist Mark Spielvogel designs and builds customized set pieces in his studio.*

*Hagley Museum*

*The Opera House set piece stood 20 feet high and 32 feet wide. It was designed with 30 gross of white lances and ignited with 30 bundles of fuses.*

much-needed heat. Smacking his gloved hands together, Howard greets Mark Spielvogel, who stands behind a table bearing a set piece he's in the throes of creating. Says Simmons, "Mark's a gifted graphics artist who designs and makes stationary sets." Stationary or set pieces are wooden frames anchored into the ground, representing designs of popular images such as the presidential portraits, the Statue of Liberty, a carousel, animals, a logo, or any facsimile desired by a client. Mark has yet to be baffled. A college graduate in studio art, drawing, and painting, Spielvogel gets right to work on a set piece once clients know what they want: "Zambelli gets all kinds of requests, and so far, we've been able to fill every one. We do by far the most set pieces of any fireworks

company anywhere. One of my proudest achievements was a show at Delaware's Hagley Museum, where I created the most complex stationary pieces ever. People are still talking about it. It took weeks to make the set pieces."

Once a client approves Mark's drawings, he transfers his sketches to graph paper, which is mathematically conveyed to a physical structure. Here is where his carpentry skills enter. "Sometimes I draw the image in chalk, from paper, right onto my worktable, so that when I begin to build the frame, I have the actual size before me." Once Spielvogel is satisfied with the wooden stationary design, he pounds peg nails into appropriate spots on the structure "to hold the lances, so that when shooters on the field

*Low-level special effects increase the show impact and utilize more of the night-sky canvas.*

© Angel Art Ltd.

*Plant superintendent Howard Simmons (right), with George Zambelli, Jr. Simmons acquires unique shells from around the world to supplement Zambelli's trademark shells and effects.*

## In Simmons's Office

A large, gentle man, Simmons fully occupies his chair in his bright office, and gestures when he talks. He loves to discuss fireworks, and especially Zambelli's, where he has worked for more than three decades. He lists his responsibilities as "Overseeing the manufacturing, fabrication, shipping, and technicians, along with helping choreograph shows. I do a lot of traveling to and from shows, too, to purchase fireworks from China, France, Brazil, Spain, and Japan. Even though we manufacture the majority of our own shells, we still buy from other countries because they may offer something special. I like to acquire unique shells, or shells that are done well by other countries. For example, China and Japan are known for manufacturing peonies and mums; France does a nice job with weeping willows and palms; while Australia is credited with making great fountains, Roman candles, and plume shells. The U.S. is recognized for manufacturing different kinds of flitters, while Zambelli does not only flitters, large multibreak shells, and spider webs, but is also famous for our crossettes and pattern shells."

light the lances, everywhere I place a nail will be visualized." Mark adds that today set pieces are complicated and challenging, especially those requiring moving parts such as his Hagley carousel, or those needing scaffolding or cranes. Some pieces require ingenuity, like forging a turning wheel. "For that, I shaped bamboo by dampening it with water to get the spinning, circular effect."

The set pieces, combined with aerial fireworks, make for incredible shows. And now, with the growing popularity of indoor shows, stationary designs are becoming even more fashionable. Mark squats at the bottom drawer of his file cabinet in his workroom. He's searching for something, and like the typical artist, he forgets time and place and is soon immersed in what lies before him.

Howard mutters, "Back to the cold. Yet in a few weeks this plant will be focused on the Fourth." But the frosty weather doesn't slow Zambelli Fireworks. Instead, the staff meet it with good cheer because it heralds the impending new year, chock full of fireworks celebrations. Simmons motions toward his office. "I work in there," he says proudly.

*Howard Simmons has worked with Zambelli for more than three decades and is George's right-hand man.*

Simmons adds, "Other countries' shells give variety to a show. Milling at foreign plants is sometimes a problem because you can get different grains. But an offsetting consideration in purchasing imported shells is the availability of certain chemicals, which some manufacturers can get more easily than others. For example, potassium perchlorate is hard to get. All fireworks manufacturers work from the same basic formulas found in the standard books. There are 'understood' standards, such as using parlon to brighten colors, or copper oxalate to get a blue hue. Zambelli is one of the few fireworks companies to have mastered a rich purple, as well as the color blue. But even with the basic 25 or 30 standard chemicals available to all fireworkers, there are still an additional seven or eight, plus what's offered in the recipes."

*Zambelli Internationale is known for having concocted one of the richest purples ever to paint the heavens.*

Having been with Zambelli Fireworks for so long, Simmons can almost read the boss's mind: "I know how George thinks, and his only major concern is that we give the best shows with quality shells at the best price. Our biggest business comes from satisfied, repeat customers who serve as ambassadors for our company, although every year we get numerous new accounts through word-of-mouth, so George is adamant about providing top-notch shows through quality powders and chemicals and a highly skilled staff."

Howard explains that when a client calls wanting a show, Zambelli charts a proposal that includes a script with suggested designs, music, and choreography that will enhance the event and fit the client's theme, budget, and show date. The nature of the display is determined after a site review and communication with state and local fire officials. "Once we've drafted a preliminary of the performance, the client sees it and suggests any changes desired. It's an ongoing exchange between them and us until they're satisfied. Then we go into high gear to fabricate and package the display. The last step is setting up and firing the show. Finally, we review the performance after the display. It is because of this conscientiousness on the part of the Zambelli staff that the company has grown so large so fast.

"In 1956 we did 17 Independence Day shows," continues Simmons. "Today we do well over 100 times that on the same day, and over 3500 shows a year. That bespeaks our reputation."

Simmons shifts in his chair, takes a phone call, then offers the reason that the company is so well respected: its highly competent workers and staff. "We train most of our workers on site, starting them out loading and handling trucks, or shipping, and—after they have more experience—we move them onto assembling displays. Before a person can be a pyrotechnician for Zambelli, he must demonstrate his knowledge and ability, either through prior experience or hands-on experience with one of our seasoned pyrotechnicians. Of course, many states now require testing and licensing of pyrotechnicians. We are proud of the dedication and safety record of our employees, from the workers at the plant to the pyrotechnician in the field."

Shooting a show is complex and begins days in advance, where technicians work on site, digging holes for the mortars; if holes can't be dug in the ground, mortar boxes with sand are used. Set pieces are assembled also. On the night of the display, in a

*Candles are angled in their racks for special effects on the Louisville Bridge.*

*Computer and software innovations take choreography to new levels. Ten or more computers are linked for larger shows.*

nonscripted, manually fired display, operators wearing goggles, fire-resistant clothing, and hard hats shuttle within the confines of the setup and the holes or racks of mortars. They dart from one area to another to load and light the explosives. The loader hustles over to the "depo" where the fireworks are stored, and then, carrying the shells, bolts to the mortars to load and reload them. Another technician—the lighter—carries a flare to ignite the shells. He and the loader must not cross paths, as a collision could result in an explosion. Once the mortar is loaded, the lighter touches the fiery flare to the safety fuse, then instantly steps back and drops to his knees to avoid the eruption that should happen within four seconds. The shell rages out of the mortar with a THUMMMMP at an incredible speed to skyrocket into the heavens, where it bursts into a profusion of colors and effects. But in a musically scripted show, both ground and aerial displays are precisely timed and executed to the show's choreography, which will be fired electronically or via the computer, and not by hand. Thus, the execution of any type of show is accomplished with unparalleled success by Zambelli Fireworks.

"So you can see how much training is needed for a display to go off without a glitch," says Simmons. "And because our company does some extraordinary things, such as firing displays atop rooftops of skyscrapers and from breakwalls, barges, and bridges, our people have to be very diversified in their training. An electronics tech, for example, must assist in many electrical shows and have significant years of training in electrical circuitry, squib wiring, and computerized firing systems before being considered appropriately trained." Simmons explains that George Sr. also expects his workers to know facts such as the chemistry of colored fire and the name and type of each of the hundreds of fireworks they make, from Zambelli Crossettes to pupidelles, spiderwebs, splitting comets, and titanium salutes.

Zambelli is acclaimed for its low number of accidents. "We've been in business for decades and decades, and just during the 30 years I've been here, there have been only three mishaps. One incident involved me. A tech was working the hydraulic press making whistles when he left the charge plate on, and it sparked. He was blown out the door and had

*Close-proximity fireworks in Baltimore, Maryland.*

we're here, though much of New Castle knows about us; they respect our privacy. Safety is, and always has been, George's number-one concern."

While safety is first with George Sr., he's credited with many other "firsts." Simmons enumerates some of them: "There are many things George introduced into the fireworks industry. One, he was preeminent in putting American black powder into foreign shells. Two, he was first in shooting fireworks off the tallest structure, and other amazing feats. And three, he was the first to design and promote safe-firing instructions and procedures. Too, he was on the leading edge when he utilized electrical firing apparatus. I'd also add that he was one of the original promoters who brought about the popularity of indoor fireworks, which are very fashionable now."

With the capabilities of doing indoor and outdoor shows, as well as manufacturing their own shells, along with being first in many areas, including the high-tech realm, where does Zambelli Internationale go from here?

Howard scratches his head. "Knowing George, I'm convinced he'll continue to be committed to his artistry and dedicated to excellence. And he'll probably want to get bigger and better." He grins. "Maybe in another 30 years from now, I'll still be here to help him do just that."

some burns, but the explosion flung a large chunk of wood into the building next to it, where I was standing talking to someone. The piece of wood slammed right into my arm, and I ended up in the hospital for four months." He shows the scarred area on his bicep.

"Most accidents," begins Simmons, "occur during the dangerous part of manufacturing—the mixing of chemicals—because the ingredients sit in their raw form. Once the shells are filled with the chemicals, they're not as volatile, though caution must be exercised. It's also the justification for having security guards on the premises, as well as an identification system, and for the isolated location of the plant. A very restricted number of people have access to the plant, and we don't advertise that

# TEN

# Fireworks Accidents and Safety

## Safety

CCORDING TO A 1994 GALLUP POLL printed in *Seventeen* magazine, 10,000 accidents are reported every year from fireworks mishaps. Of that number, 2,500 result in eye injuries and vision loss, and nearly all the rest in burns and other related impairments. Considering that a simple handheld sparkler reaches a temperature (1,800 degrees) hot enough to melt gold, it is easy to understand how burns can happen.

Imagine, then, what kinds of burns would result from misfired shells, errant rockets, or other harmful fireworks. Fingers and hands blown off, eyes gouged out, or clothes aflame are only some of the horrors associated with fireworks accidents. And many of these kinds of misfortunes did occur when the art of pyrotechnics wasn't regulated. Since 9/11, however, fireworks and other types of explosives are some of the most rigidly controlled substances, which resulted from both a concern for safety and the government's interest in knowing who possesses and transports explosives.

Though the accounting for hazardous materials can be a hassle for pyrotechnics companies, Zambelli's excellent recordkeeping system permits the location of a grain of powder in an instant. George Sr. heralds the strict government regulations: "The rules eliminate perpetrators of crime and other illegal and dangerous activities in our business. If a company—like ours—remains above board, there's no problem." George doesn't fret over the endless documents and regulations because his fireworks business has the best insurance rating of all the 150-plus in existence. "We achieve this," he says, "not only by following the rules but also by taking those extra steps in safeguarding others."

*George Sr. and his younger brother, Lou, inspecting shells in the early 1960s. Safety has been important from the very beginning.*

# Safety History Record

The background of pyrotechnics and safety is relatively short, as it wasn't until the 1930s that the first antifireworks movement took hold in response to the numerous injuries incurred from cherry bombs, Roman candles, and a host of other types of fireworks devices. The discovery of potassium chlorate in 1840 brought about some of the most serious fireworks mishaps because of its power to ignite with sulfur. The Gunpowder Act of 1860 advocated safety practices, while the Explosives Acts of 1875 and 1895 forbade the use of chlorate (especially potassium chlorate) and sulfur mixtures. During that time, the first restrictive law was written. It prohibited the majority of the different types of fireworks from being sold to the general public. It was rewritten several times before it reached its present state, and the prohibition holds true today. Still, from 1903 to 1915 an estimated 43,000 people were injured and nearly 900 killed in fireworks accidents on or around the Fourth of July. This brought about and emphasized the "Safe and Sane Fourth" movement in 1910, with enforcing legislation following shortly after.

In the mid-1960s, governing agencies prohibited the manufacture and sale of M-80s (similar to hand grenades), cherry bombs (red 1" spheres), and silver salutes (silver cylinders with a fuse extending from its side). These types of fireworks carried 25 to 40 times more explosives than usual. By 1976, during the nation's bicentennial celebration, emergency rooms across the nation reported 11,000 fireworks injuries. Thus the Consumer Product Safety Commission (CPSC), with the APA (American Pyrotechnic Association), enacted

national standards and regulations for the manufacturing and labeling of pyrotechnics, along with stipulations that only enough firecracker powder to cover one's fingertip could be sold; that fuses must burn long enough to allow operators time to get away before detonation; and that new fireworks must be tested before being marketed.

Of course, once such bans are placed on what was formerly lawful, a black market opens. This is exactly what happened with fireworks. The Internet often serves as a black market, as do shops selling firecrackers from basement holdings, and other unsavory locales or methods. A case in point is illustrated by the CPSC's lawsuit against Shelton Wholesale Inc. and Polaris Fireworks Inc.[8] for importing and distributing more than 3.5 million banned or mislabeled fireworks that had been disallowed because of their high rate of malfunction and erratic explosion. The lawsuit charged that the two companies had been warned and penalized by the CPSC over four years for dealing in illegal contraband.

Enmeshing oneself in fireworks enterprises is a costly and serious business. There are expenses for licensing and for properly storing powders and other similar products. For example, the making of black powder, gunpowder, flash powder, or such components as stars, as well as the testing, storing, selling, and detonating of explosives, along with performing pyrotechnics shows, or setting off firecrackers, require licenses . . . or are otherwise illegal. To get licensed, one must be at least 21 years old, free of criminal, drug, fugitive, or insanity charges, and have storage facilities (magazines, bunkers) constructed to specified measurements and materials. One must also pass tests for certification and/or licensing. Other requisites must be fulfilled, too, depending on the state to which application is being made, and may involve fingerprinting, photographing, medical authorization, and obtaining a certificate of insurance, along with filling out forms in duplicate and triplicate. Reading and memorizing endless BATF (Bureau of Alcohol, Tobacco, and Firearms) documents, booklets, and pamphlets, are also required.

To offset felonious fireworks acts, a number of agencies have been established to regulate the manufacture, storage, sale, and display of explosives. Additionally, these agencies can make random spot inspections. Such agencies include:

**BATF:** The Bureau of Alcohol, Tobacco, and Firearms tracks down illegal users and stolen goods and attempts to seek out secret manufacturers of fireworks. This federal agency also monitors the storage and transportation of such products.

**DOT:** Department of Transportation, another federal agency, regulates the storage and movement of hazardous materials. Although classification of explosives under this organization used to employ the designations Class A, Class B, and Class C, classification now categorizes explosives as 1.3G, UN0335 (display fireworks, which formerly were called Class B), and 1.4G, UN0336 (consumer fireworks, which used to be tagged as Class C explosives). For theatrical or indoor effects, 1.4G or 1.4S and 2.6.3 are often used; Class A explosives are now part of the Division 1.1. classification.

**OSHA:** The federal Office of Safety and Health Administration inspects fireworks plants and regulates worker safety, training, and other related aspects.

**NFPA:** The National Fire Protection Agency looks into separation distances (i.e., the distance of one magazine to another), how much explosive is on the grounds, and so on.

**EPA:** The Environmental Protection Agency keeps tabs on the storage of hazardous chemicals.

In addition, a universe of other governing bodies oversees the intricacies of fireworks; these include the Fire Marshals Association of North America, the American Pyrotechnical Association (for professional fireworks exhibitors, manufacturers, retailers, and importers), the National Society for the Prevention of Blindness, the Consumer Product Safety Commission, the Pyrotechnics Guild International for amateur pyrotechnicians, and others.

In general, fireworks are safe. Compared with other forms of danger from fire or fire-related sources, fireworks have the lowest accident incidence. Mishaps resulting from ovens and cooking ranges average 43,000 per year; from gasoline and other fuels, 28,000; from stoves and space heaters, 27,000; from chimneys and fireplaces, 23,000; from cigarettes and lighters, about 15,000; and from outdoor grills, 14,000. Yearly, fireworks accidents average 11,000. This low figure results from strict regulation and constant oversight.

So fireworks today are a protected business because of restrictions requiring the possession of safer chemicals, smaller amounts of explosives, clearer warnings and labeling, better fuses, precise transportation routes, and enforced training and licensing. Additionally, other requirements include the truck fueling before loading fireworks; prohibiting fireworks from being left alone at a display site; the inspection of each shell to make sure the quick match is in place; the checking and rechecking of mortars and shells; the attendance of firefighters at shows; the delay of electric power to shells until needed; the presence of at least one experienced pyrotechnician as supervisor; and the proximity of other fireworkers at shows in positions of supply tenders, spotters, monitors, and so on.

# A History of Fireworks Accidents

No matter how much caution is exercised during a fireworks show, misfortunes do happen to even the most conscientious and circumspect in the business, though Zambelli Internationale has been fortunate in this regard.

George Zambelli, Sr., says, "The death, years ago, of my brother-in-law in the plant was a real loss, though even today we don't know what he was doing to have set off the explosion; some say he moved a ladder, creating a spark that exploded everything in the storage shed. And an employee was killed when he carelessly leaned over a mortar, and the shell fired. There also have been a few errant firecrackers that emitted fallout and other hot powders. The recent English Avenue plant explosion is another accident of which we don't know the cause. But all in all, that's about the extent of our accidents . . . and thank God for that. Yes, we've been lucky, but we've also been extraordinarily careful, too."

Some fireworks companies have experienced such devastating accidents—with a loss not only of facilities, but of family members as well—that they never get back on their feet again. Says George, "When another company undergoes that, I try to be right there to help in some way. Because my company has been blessed so far doesn't mean we won't be a victim some day. I know if that ever happened, I would want the help of my fireworks colleagues and friends."

Some of the most famous historical accidents include:[9]

**1720:** Because of carelessness of a customer, John Brock (expert fireworker) died from severe burns, as did his daughter after 22 days.

**1722:** One Mr. Goodsleaf was making fireworks

when one went ablaze, blowing him up, and setting fire to his home and a house adjoining it.

**1749:** The 1748 peace treaty signing at Aix-la-Chappelle was celebrated throughout major European cities, but London featured a 410-foot-long and 114-foot-high wooden temple, housing 10,650 rockets, shells, and pinwheels and 100 brass cannons. A disagreement between firemaster Ruggieri and other staff members resulted in an explosion and fire that, when finally put out, had exhausted everyone, leaving no one wanting to see the fireworks.

**1824:** Fireworker nailing shut a case of rockets in a plant caused a spark, blowing up the plant and killing two.

**1852:** A fireworker was blown to pieces while preparing a "hot" mercury mixture.

**1858:** An explosion at Madame Coton's fireworks plant resulted in her death and injuries to 300.

**1859:** Explosion at a factory killed three during the initial blast, and three later.

**1866:** An Independence Day celebration was in progress when someone threw a firecracker over a fence in a boat yard, causing a pile of wood shavings to explode and flames to jump from rooftop to rooftop, block to block, making the city a pile of charred ruins and leaving 10,000 homeless.

**Late 1800s:** Fireworks became common celebratory finales, with numerous deaths and injuries accompanying them, so much so that by this time, Independence Day had become known as "Death's Busy Day." From 1875 through 1892, 28 more accidents occurred from chlorate and sulfur mixtures, resulting in an additional 11 fatalities.

**1885:** A workman in a Mitcham factory pounded a nail into a box containing composition, creating sparks that set rockets flying in all directions. A massive fire raged, but only two injuries resulted

because of the implementation of the Explosives Act of 1875.

**1885:** Ten fireworkers were killed and 20 injured in an Italian factory explosion.

**1889:** In France, an explosion of red phosphorus and potassium chlorate killed seven girls.

**1900–1930:** During this 30-year period, more than 4,000 people died while manufacturing fireworks, watching displays, or playing with them.

**1902:** In Madison Square Garden in New York a shell predetonated, killing 15 and injuring 8 seriously.

**1902:** New York newspaper publisher William Hearst had planned a major fireworks extravaganza to celebrate his election to Congress. But instead of sinking huge mortars into the ground, the workers just set them on top. When the first mortar was lit, it didn't propel the shell into the air, but instead the shell exploded inside the mortar and set off a chain reaction that detonated all 59 other mortars, hurtling shells into crowds, causing burns and shock waves. Eighteen were killed, more than 80 were wounded, and windows were shattered all around Madison Square Park. Victims' families sued Hearst.

**1904:** As a joke, a girl in Priceburg, Pennsylvania, threw a squib into a closed stove and killed seven women, with others bearing countless injuries.

**1904:** In a Camden, New Jersey, plant, a worker accidentally touched a mixing instrument, with trace potassium chlorate on it, to sulfur and caused a heinous explosion, killing one-fifth of the workers.

**1904:** A Findlay, Ohio, plant exploded; 12 died, 12 were injured, and two were reported missing—all out of a workforce of 30.

**1904:** On the third floor of a Philadelphia fireworks factory, an explosion resulted when young girls were packing fireworks; only two of 22 girls were accounted for.

**1915:** In Germany, a pyrotechnics munitions factory exploded; the number of victims never became public.

**1930:** In Devon, Pennsylvania, spontaneous ignition in a fireworks magazine destroyed everything as well as raining down a cloud of debris, sending shock waves and noise for nearly 80 miles around, setting houses on fire, derailing and wrecking a passing train, and killing 15, as well as injuring and burning many more.

**1931:** A local drugstore serving the 5,000 residents of Spencer, Iowa, sold stacks of fireworks in its basement for the Fourth of July. Two preteen boys lit sparklers, accidentally dropping one into a box of cherry bombs. Everything blew and smoked, fire spread from one floor to the next, from building to building, destroying businesses, rows of houses, the American Legion hall, and town structures. Water pressure died and the wind shifted, setting other buildings afire. Only a counter-fire sucking the oxygen out of the raging inferno put an end to the devastation. In the final accounting, 75 businesses and offices were ravaged and tons of valuable records and inventory were lost or totally destroyed, with millions of dollars in damages.

**1936:** A young girl in Ramsen, Iowa, was playing with sparklers near a tent set up for the Fourth of July. She dropped a glowing rod into oil-soaked rags. The fire spread to the tent, leaped the walls of a garage, and raged for hours, causing the loss of half the town and leaving 100 homeless.

**1936:** In Oyens, Iowa, a town of 100 near Ramsen (and on the same day as the fire described above), a firecracker was thrown into an empty lot of dry grass and set a city block aflame. But since the town was too small to have a fire department, and the surrounding communities that did have firefighters were at the Ramsen fire, no one was available to put out what started as a small blaze. The town burned.

**1981:** In London, for the royal wedding of Prince Charles and Lady Diana Spencer, a fireworks show was patterned after the 1749 Aix-la-Chappelle celebration, duplicating everything, right down to the firetrucks and huge temple. But instead of recreating a 3-D temple akin to the one at Aix-la-Chapelle, England had created a 2-D cardboard structure. The fireworks didn't go off, so the firetrucks resorted to waving hoses at a nonexistent fire for effect.[10]

**1983:** Missing and dead were two employees in an explosion at a New York fireworks plant. The explosion caused massive destruction, huge mushroom clouds of chemicals, whizzing mortars, blown-out windows, waves of flash heat, piercing whistles and noises, and rumbling, shaking floors.[11]

**1995:** A California fireworks plant employee was killed when a trailer he was loading exploded.[12]

**1997:** Four employees were killed when a display company's storage facility blew up in Tennessee.

**1997:** Eight commercial fireworks customers were killed in a small city in Ohio when an individual tossed something lit into a building where fireworks were sold.

**1998:** In Independence, Ohio, a young female spectator attending a Fourth of July fireworks celebration was killed when a shell struck her in the head.

Of course, nonexplosive fireworks mishaps here also occurred, such as the case of a man who lost his balance when a firecracker went off, causing him to fall into a pond and drown; a girl who was hit by an errant rocket, setting her clothes afire; a boy who jumped at the sound of a firecracker and fell out of a tree and died; and a man who while building a temple and assembling the fireworks for it, fell from the top of the temple and died.

"The U.S. Consumer Product Safety Commission (CPSC) estimates that in 1998, 8,500 people were treated in hospital emergency rooms for injuries associated with fireworks. . . . 6,300 injuries . . . in 1999."[13] The May 16, 2000, edition of *World Socialist Web Site* reported an explosion in a Dutch warehouse that killed more than 20 people and injured 600-plus. Several of the bodies went unidentified.[14] A March 2001 report stated that dozens of Asian-Pacific children, aged eight and under, were killed or maimed while assembling fireworks in an unlicensed facility as a way of "boosting income." The death toll ranged between 37 and 60 children and four adults, and the blast destroyed several rooms.[15] In a South American country, an early-morning firecracker destroyed a 2002 New Year celebration when it sparked a blaze that engulfed numerous fireworks stands on streets where vendors were set up, killing nearly 300 people. In December 2002, *North Kitsap Fire Rescue* reported a hillside blaze ignited by illegal fireworks that was snuffed out by 500 gallons of firefighting foam; injuries were reported.[16] A 2003 CNN report stated that a Dutch arsonist set fire to an illegal fireworks depot, flattening an entire neighborhood, killing a couple dozen residents and injuring hundreds.[17] Another 2003 report, this one by an AP writer, detailed a succession of fireworks explosions that blasted through crowds in a central market, destroying businesses and vendor stands and killing 41 with an additional 50 unaccounted for.

The list goes on.

Today, in the U.S., there are so few fireworks mishaps—because of stringent rules and regulations—that when one does occur, even a minor one, it makes instant news. According to the National Council on Fireworks Safety,[18] "Injuries

*Lou shows George III special manufacturing safety techniques.*

per 100,000 pounds of fireworks have dropped from 38.3 in 1976 to 10.1 in 1995. . . ." Still, that shouldn't stop any fireworker from practicing the highest safety standards for himself and others. The publication "Fireworks in America" offers the following advice: "Fireworks are not toys. . . . Illegal explosive devices can kill or maim you. There is a serious problem each year with the illegal production and sale of . . . 'M-80s,' 'silver salutes,' 'blockbusters,' 'quarter-pounders'. . . . These items will not contain a manufacturer's name and are usually unlabeled. Don't purchase or use unlabeled fireworks . . . . Homemade fireworks are deadly. Never attempt to make your own fireworks and do not purchase any kits that are advertised for making fireworks. Mixing and loading chemical powders is very dangerous and can kill or seriously injure you."[19]

The beauty of fireworks will never be an issue, but their safety will always remain a concern.

# ELEVEN

# Family Album

———————— ✦ ————————

**L**IKE JANUS, WHO LOOKS BACKWARD as well as glances forward, George Sr. takes a moment to relax and reflect. He understands that he has one foot firmly entrenched in the past, and the other foot alighting on the future, and somewhere in between he must find a happy medium. He looks around at his wife, children, and grandchildren and whispers, "This is that happy medium." He knows he would not be the success he is today if it wasn't for his wife and children. Right now, reminiscences fill his mind, and he looks back at his past with a smile. "We've had our troubles but our good times, too. None of the success from my business would have any meaning if the Lord hadn't blessed me with my wife and kids. He laughs when he tells about the time he found one of Marcy's high school report card 30 years after she graduated, tucked inside a *World Book* encyclopedia volume that he had randomly picked to read. "When I called to her and then held up the brown-tinged paper before her, she sheepishly smiled, saying 'If it took you 30 years to find that, Dad, I guess I hid it pretty good.' I had to laugh."

He also looks back on an incident when his five children tried to kidnap their mother for her birthday to take her to the casinos. When George Sr. found out, he asked, "'When are we leaving?' I was afraid I would miss out on something." In a *Pittsburgh Post Gazette* interview in its December 29, 1990 "Dossier" section, George reveals some of his personal secrets—such as his love for ice cream, his always dreaming of driving a convertible with a chauffeur's cap on, and, if he could, playing Michael Douglas in a movie. When asked what he could most do without, he laughingly answers, "Lectures from my daughters."

Not only a family man, George Sr. is also a religious one. July 13, 1998, in an article by Charlotte Faltermayer in the issue of *Time* magazine, George Sr. offers a reflection about the dangers of his job, "[I'm] dealing with explosives. . . . It's like a battlefield. Anything can happen." His belief in God is what keeps him doing it. During a 2002 exhibiting of his famous "Thunder Over Louisville" show, the *Courier-Journal* of Louisville, Kentucky, commented that before the show, George attended mass at the Cathedral of the Assumption, saying, "I pray for a good, safe show . . . . We're dealing with 60 tons of explosives tonight. We need the help of a power a whole lot higher than me."

A loving man, a brilliant and creative one, a classy one, a religious one, and a compassionate one—there is little more one can ask for in a single package. His wife and children appreciate and dedicate themselves to the sometimes preoccupied, occasionally grumpy, but always adorable package.

*A remarkably handsome and imposing George Zambelli Sr. smiles for his New Castle High School graduation in May 1942. He already knew what his career would be, and was eager to ignite it and push ahead.*

They're the ones who wrap the beautiful bows around him.

In summing up his life, George admits he'd have to check his journal to name all of the many dignitaries he has met, entertained, or was entertained by. Nearly every U.S. president since JFK, royalty from numerous every countries, and prime ministers from around the world have been energized by George Zambelli the man and his shows. He and his family have traveled each land and each corner of the globe—and always under joy and under grace where as guests in multinational cities greet them with awards. Some of those awards mean so much to him that he can whip them off his tongue without looking at his walls covered with plaques and frames. "I was one of the first inductees into the International Festivals & Events Association/Miller Brewing Co. Hall of Fame, and my family as a whole has been honored with the

*George and Connie love to spend time with their grandchildren prior to lighting the skies, as seen in this 1998 picture. (Back Row): George III, Alison holding Alandra, Connie, George Sr., Summer; (Front Row): Constance, Aubriana, Jared, Michael Jr.*

Western Pennsylvania Family Business of the Year Award, and has received acknowledgments from the Family Enterprise Center and the Family Firm Institute, among many other awards."

Though the Zambellis like to receive such honors, they prefer to give instead, as seen in their support of the University of Pittsburgh Cancer Institute, the Dream Makers of Children's Hospital of Pittsburgh, educational causes, and an exhibit underway at the Detroit Parade Museum—among many other Zambelli philanthropic projects. People who know the family say that they're always helping some individual, cause, or organization, but yet they never boast about it. This must be the test of true character, for not one member of the Zambellis steps forward and tries to take credit for what they all do. And George hasn't forgotten old friends or acquaintances who have helped him in the past; in turn, he helps them. Never does he let a promise he made to another go by, or fail to greet his staff and

say a few kind words to the people who are so dedicated to him. One would think that the seasoned executive of a large international fireworks corporation would be as tough on the inside as he appears on the outside. The opposite is true. He's forever trying *not* to hurt anyone's feelings, including those of his own family, who are more important to him than all of his thousands of clients rolled together. Family glue is the stuff that makes them stick together through the good and the bad, the easy and the hard, the agony and the pain, the simple and the complex, and the love and . . . . the love. He flourishes on his family, is animated by it, and is mellowed from it.

Though sometimes a deep, roaring, laughter will erupt from his belly, it's more frequently an impish grin when the family plays jokes on him. George remarks, "My memories are sweet, and they are many." He recalls how Danabeth (his youngest) always teasingly makes a big deal at family functions to have him announce that she is his favorite child. His eyes sparkle. "Always the children and grandchildren tease me . . . and I love it." He tells about an instance when he was driving a minivan to Detroit and it was loaded with boxes of Zambelli chocolates that George gives only to his clients. In the back seat the girls and George Jr. made sounds as though they were tearing open the boxes and eating the candy. "My children made my head whip around so fast it looked like a top. We all got a good laugh out of it and, still, all throughout the trip they teased me, especially when I took a wrong turn, and they all the more took joy in kidding me."

As fine a father as he is with his children, he is

equally as good with his grandchildren, even allowing them to do things he wouldn't have let his own children do decades ago—such as allowing to tell Michael Jr. dumb blonde jokes, especially when his mother is a blonde; or letting the young grandkids crawl up onto his lap to tell stories, sing to him, and read to him; or having the girls bring him their dolls or give him blow-by-blow descriptions of their school day. The older grandchildren know how to give him a certain smile or push a hidden button to make him melt and give in. With them, his patience is endless.

*Endless. Time:* The strokes of a clock are important to George, as they count down his past and push forward his future—one that he tussles with daily in his battle with lymphoma and multiple myeloma, as well as his previous incidents of pneumonia and other illnesses that normally would take their toll on anyone, let alone a 78-year old man. *Time:* He makes the best of it. On his and his wife's 50th anniversary, he took all of his 21 immediate family members on a Caribbean cruise. Rarely does he take off work for fun but as he ages he seems to want to get his priorities straight, and first with him are his loved ones who work together and play together. Every one of the Zambelli children and grandchildren are involved in the business in some manner. They all toil as a single entity to meet the patriarch's demands, much the same way drones work for the honcho of a bee colony . . . And they have fun doing it!

**Says George, "We are parts of a whole—a single unit: my family, excellent staff and a secret formula that masterfully combines family and business with imagination and technology, which is now being handed down to the grandchildren.**

George sees that while his old-fashioned ways are being replaced by high technology, he welcomes it, knowing that his time has passed. Although he'll always be the "main man" in the business, he's also stepping aside to make room for the future generation. George may not be any computer whiz but he knows how to get what he wants and needs . . . a determination, an energy, and a business ingenuity that has allowed him to go find the latest and greatest in multimillion-dollar computer wizardry for setting up electronic choreography and synchronized firing, as well as formulating database inventories and cutting-edge scripting techniques. Though George strongly believes competition is healthy, the Zambellis have always been in the vanguard of the business through computerization. Offers George, "No other fireworks company has what we have, in terms of staff, equipment, facilities, warehousing, firing technology, and computerization." And no sooner do they update their hardware, software and other equipment than they're off learning about something more leading-edge, or buying intellectual property that's just been released

*Taken at George Sr.'s family-owned restaurant, "The Grand Finale," in his office building—the Z Penn Center—this 2003 picture shows workers, associates, and friends as they pause for their daily lunch, a 40-year old practice.*

*"A Sweet Man."* George Sr. always enjoys treating his friends and clients to his world-famous homemade Zambelli chocolates. His children liked to tease him into thinking they were eating the candy reserved only for special people.

and promises to be newer and better. And while George sees the value in technology, his old traditional self believes that no computerized virtual reality will ever replace live fireworks shows because no machine can engender human emotions—like those feelings that wrap tightly around a spectator when his heart is jolted by the sound of a boom, or when his eyes take in so much color at once that he is left speechless and motionless, overwhelmed for one brief stretch of minutes in a pyrotechnical fantasia. "Fireworks are a family activity; they're magic, and they take us back to the good times of our childhood and make us feel good about ourselves, if only for that moment," he says with a nod. Today, fireworks are shot more than ever at baseball and football games, theme parks, fairs, galas, weddings, grand openings, and on and on." For over 100 years the Zambellis have reveled in the glee of others when they light up a sky, and they plan on continu-

ing that tradition. "Our past has been fireworks, our present is fireworks, and our future is fireworks. That is who we are. My children say they can never replace me. Well, if they can't, then I'm the one who failed them. Besides, for us, fireworks are fun, and made safer and more easily handled through high-tech, so I know the family will carry on our love for a long time more."

Does George's future encompass projects he has on the drawing board—projects he works on from the moment he wakes to the moment the sun sets, or is he now considering slowing down, passing the mantle on to his younger ones? "As long as I can breathe, think, and move, I'll be here." He looks over his shoulder, adding, "I don't think I'll ever be able to say I've accomplished everything I've dreamed of, and what I have done has been done with family, love, joy, and the good Lord. Doing this book has stirred some bittersweet memories for my wife and me. Gathering all the photos and information spanning a century was not only a major undertaking but it was also the catalyst to remind us of our past and to thrust us into the future. I have no regrets. I'm the most blessed man in the world. Look at all the love in my family. How could anyone ask for more?" He puts his arm around his wife Connie's shoulder and grins. "She's been at my side for over 58 years. She's guided me, supported me, and encouraged me, and she raised our children to be just like that. That's why I say, 'Who could ask for more?'"

Closing this chapter of his life, George turns the page to the future. He'll never quit fireworks . . . and maybe he'll even outlive them. He smiles that endearing smirk. "I never stop learning. I won't rust out, I'll wear out."

So, like George, turn the next page, and enjoy the Zambellis' reminiscences in this photo album.

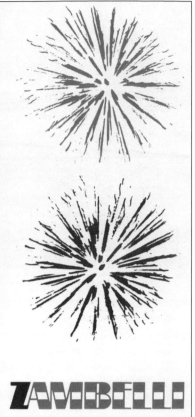

**FIREWORKS MANUFACTURING COMPANY, INC.**

P. O. Boxes 801 and 1463, New Castle, Pennsylvania 16103 • 299 N. W. 52nd Terrace, Suite 118, Boca Raton, Florida 33432
Telephones: (New Castle, Code 412) 652-5711, 652-6220, 658-6611 • (Boca Raton, Code 305) 994-1588

*This sample reflects the addition of the Boca Raton office and indicates the age and size of the company, called Zambelli Fireworks Manufacturing Company, Inc. at that time.*

**U.S. Corporate Headquarters**
P.O. Box 1463
New Castle, Pennsylvania 16103
(412) 658-6611 or (800) 245-0397
FAX (412) 658-8318

**INTERNATIONALE**
**FIREWORKS MANUFACTURING COMPANY, INC. -** *SINCE 1893*

*Red-and-white block letters have been changed to a solid, rich red that shouts out the company's name. In addition to the New Castle headquarters, and the Boca Raton office, there is now a western region added as the corporation keeps growing. Also the word "Internationale" has been added.*

*An early version of a Zambelli brochure. Notice the red-and-white block lettering. The sketches of the fireworks on the simple brochure will later be replaced by contemporary, high-tech images.*

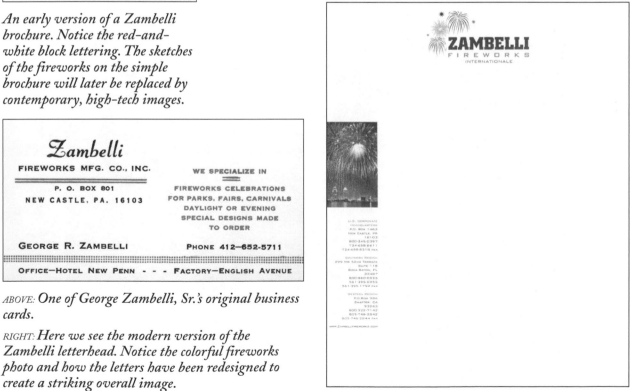

*Zambelli*

FIREWORKS MFG. CO., INC.

P. O. BOX 801
NEW CASTLE, PA. 16103

GEORGE R. ZAMBELLI

WE SPECIALIZE IN

FIREWORKS CELEBRATIONS
FOR PARKS, FAIRS, CARNIVALS
DAYLIGHT OR EVENING
SPECIAL DESIGNS MADE
TO ORDER

PHONE 412—652-5711

OFFICE—HOTEL NEW PENN - - - FACTORY—ENGLISH AVENUE

*ABOVE: One of George Zambelli, Sr.'s original business cards.*

*RIGHT: Here we see the modern version of the Zambelli letterhead. Notice the colorful fireworks photo and how the letters have been redesigned to create a striking overall image.*

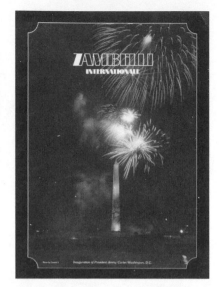

The Zambelli Bros., as they were referred to at the time, presented the history of fireworks in this earliest brochure. It was written by George R. Zambelli, Jr., M.D., demonstrating how active all family members are no matter what their career is.

This succeeding brochure introduces a new company name, Zambelli Fireworks Mfg. Co., Inc. It contains a written account of the history of their fireworks business, and details the active roles of many of the Zambelli family in the company.

Having grown, and exhibited shows across the globe, the company adopted the name, Zambelli Internationale, and created a new business logo, asillustrated on the cover of this late 1970s catalog.

By 1979, the company was recognized as Zambelli . . . The First Family of Fireworks. *The title is used on company correspondence, as shown on this promotional mailer with reply card.*

*Expansion of the company in the early 1980s led to two new offices. As depicted on this company advertisement, the southern Florida and western California regional offices were opened to support the U.S. corporate head-quarters in New Castle, PA.*

*Presidential displays have become a tradition for the Zambellis. Here Zambelli . . . The First Family of Fireworks, paints the sky above the White House for president Reagan and guests at one of the annual Congressional picnics.*

*The Italian Times published an article on Zambelli Fireworks, profiling the Italian family's roots and pride, and honoring the Zambellis of yesterday and today.*

*This early 1900s brochure high-lights a moment in time from the National Victory Celebration (Desert Storm troop return) when Zambelli Fireworks brilliantly lit the skies over Washington, D.C.*

*This recent Zambelli brochure details their history, discusses how Zambelli has changed the face of fireworks through their tradition of excellence, and most importantly describes "The Zambelli Touch."*

*The 2003 tri-fold brochure.*

The gang's all here! Mugging for the camera in the 1940s are the Zambelli men after a church service. The proud father, Antonio, and his sons were very close and worked together as a "dynamite" team. (Left to right): George Sr., Carmen, Antonio (Dad and company founder), Joseph, and Louis.

This is a classic photo featuring the parents of George's wife, Connie's. Left to right: George, daughter Marcy, Connie, her mother, Mary, and her father, Felix Thomas. This was taken around 1976 at a local fair featuring a display of George's fireworks.

*Family couch potatoes? George Sr. relaxes with some of his grandchildren prior to one of the biggest and most well-known pyrotechnics extragavanzas: "Thunder Over Louisville." Left to right: Aubriana, Anna Jane (family friend), Constance (on George Sr.'s lap), Michael Jr., and Jared.*

*George and Connie were honored at the Mercer Raceway Park's 'Night of Fire,' a tribute to the master. Michael Jr. and Constance proudly stand with their grandparents after a magnificent display.*

*George Sr. and Connie were the first honorees titled "the Generade and the Miller's Maiden" at Carnevale—a masked ball presented by the Historical Society of Western Pennsylvania.*

*This photo appeared in the U.S. News and World Report periodical "Amazing Families". Back row from left: Annlyn, George Jr., Donnalou, Marcy and Danabeth. Middle row: Amberlee, Connie (holding Jared), George Sr. and Jessica. Front row: Alison, George III and Summer.*

*"It All Ends with Z." A great way to end a book about the internationally famous Zambelli family is to let them show their climb to success from their early days at the bottom to their present-day 'top-of-the-world' position as suggested by this photo. Starting from the bottom rung are Danabeth and family, Annlyn and family, Marcy and family, Donnalou and family, and approaching the top balcony are George Jr. and family, and finally Connie and George Sr., overseeing their brood. This 1996 photo was taken on a cruise in celebration of Mom and Dad's 50th wedding anniversary.*

# TWELVE

# Sparkling Fireworks Recipes

## ENJOY A PYROTECHNIC DISPLAY WITH A TASTY DISH FROM A ZAMBELLI FAMILY RECIPE

## *New Year's—January ("New Year's Confetti Shells")*

### FIREWORKS PIZZA
*(Everyone's favorite)*

1   purchased Italian bread shell (16 oz.) or baked 12" pizza crust
1   jar (12 oz.) pickled Giardiniera vegetable mix, well drained
1   tbsp. chopped drained pepperoncini peppers
1   cup crumbled feta cheese
2   tsp. chopped fresh parsley (or 1 tsp. dried parsley flakes)

Heat oven to 400 degrees. Place bread shell on ungreased cookie sheet. Arrange vegetable mix and peppers evenly over bread shell. Sprinkle with cheese and parsley. Bake 10-12 minutes or until cheese is melted and bubbly. Makes 8 servings.

# ITALIAN FESTIVAL TOMATO SAUCE

*(to go with Fireworks Pizza)*

1 can (28 oz.) whole Italian-style tomatoes, drained
1 can (28 oz.) Italian-style tomato purée
2 cloves garlic, crushed
2 tsp. chopped fresh parsley (or 1 tsp. dried parsley flakes)
2 tsp. crushed onion
   Enough olive or vegetable oil to coat bottom of pan
½ tsp. salt
½ tsp. pepper
1 tsp. sugar
   Italian cheese blend (Romano, Parmesan, etc.)

Place crushed tomatoes, tomato purée, and parsley in blender; blend until smooth. Pour oil into pan. Heat with garlic and onion. Add tomato mixture, along with salt, pepper, and sugar. Sprinkle in the blend of Italian cheeses (if you prefer, sprinkle cheese on the cooked, sauced dish). Heat to boil and simmer on low for approximately 1 hour.

# NEW YEAR'S DAY ESCAROLE AND BEANS

*(George Sr.'s favorite)*

1 cup chicken broth
1 large head escarole (well washed and
   coarsely cut)
2 tbsp. olive oil

2 garlic cloves, minced
1 15 oz. can cannellini beans
4 fresh basil leaves, cut up

In a large saucepan, place chicken broth and escarole, bring to a boil, and simmer for an hour. In another saucepan, gently brown the garlic in oil, then add beans with their liquid, and heat thoroughly. Combine with escarole mixture and let simmer for 10-12 minutes. Stir carefully with wooden spoon. This should have a soupy consistency (add a little more broth or water, if necessary). This is excellent with hot pepper flakes, grated cheese, and hot Italian bread.

# PARTY WHITE CONFETTI CAKE

*(A confetti, horns, and hats celebration)*

*Cake*

2¼  cups cake flour

2  tsp. baking powder

½  tsp. salt

¾  cup margarine

1½  tsp. vanilla

1½  cups sugar

2¾  cups milk

4  egg whites beaten to stiffness (but not dry)

Combine flour, baking powder, and salt. Add sugar, and cream the mixture until fluffy. Add milk, vanilla, and dry ingredients, beating until smooth. Gently fold egg whites into batter until thoroughly blended. Divide batter evenly into 2 greased-and-floured 9 x 1½ round layer cake pans. Bake at 350 degrees, about 35-40 minutes. Cool. Refrigerate cake when done.

*Frosting*

1  small box vanilla instant pudding and pie filling mix

1½  cups milk

Stir above together. Set aside. Place one layer of cake on serving plate and spread all of pudding on it; this is the bottom layer. Place second layer of cake on top of bottom layer. Cover with Cream Cheese Frosting. Decorate with confetti sprinkles.

## CREAM CHEESE FROSTING

1  3-oz. pkg. cream cheese

¼  cup milk or cream

2½  cups confectioners' sugar

1  tsp. vanilla extract

Soften cream cheese with part of the milk. Add confectioners' sugar and the balance of milk. Add vanilla until thoroughly blended. Frost cake and top it with sprinkles.

# February—Valentine's Day ("Heart-Shell Bomb")

## A VALENTINE'S ROUSING RICH RICOTTA CAKE
*(Connie's favorite)*

*Topping*
- 1 small box vanilla instant pudding
- 1 cup milk
- 9 oz. Cool Whip

Blend all ingredients.

*Cake*

- 1 box strawberry cake mix
- ¾ cup sugar
- 4 eggs

- 1 tsp. vanilla
- 2 lb. ricotta cheese
- 1 carton of strawberries

Beat together all ingredients except strawberries. Pour into greased oblong cake pan. Bake in 350-degree oven for 55-60 minutes. Arrange strawberries on top of cake.

## "HEART"-Y EGGPLANT PARMIGIANA
*(Lovers' choice)*

- 2 medium eggplants
- ⅓ cup milk
- ½ cup seasoned bread crumbs
- ½ cup vegetable oil
- 1 tsp. fresh or dried parsley

- 1 cup grated Parmesan cheese
- 1 cup mozzarella cheese
  Sauce (Italian Festival Tomato Sauce, page 137, or your own or a purchased sauce.)

Peel eggplant and cut crosswise into slices. Dip slices into milk and coat with bread crumbs. Heat oil in nonstick skillet over medium heat. Cook eggplant slices 2 minutes on each side or until golden brown.

Spread ¾ cup of sauce in ungreased rectangular baking dish. Arrange half of the eggplant slices over sauce. Sprinkle with ½ cup of Parmesan cheese and ½ cup of shredded mozzarella cheese. Layer remaining eggplant, then top with ½ cup sauce or remaining cheeses. Bake about 20 minutes at 350 degrees or until cheese is bubbly.

# March—St. Patrick's Day
## ("Green and Gold Flittering Circles")

## PADDY'S SPRING SHAMROCK CAKE
*(Applauding spring and "green")*

*Cake*

| | |
|---|---|
| 1 box yellow cake mix | 1 tsp. vanilla |
| 3 cups sifted flour | ¾ cup margarine |
| 2½ tsp. baking powder | 1½ cups sugar |
| 1 tsp. salt | 3 eggs |

Mix and beat together the following ingredients until fluffy: margarine, sugar, eggs, vanilla. Grease and flour 8 x 10 baking dish. Pour batter into baking dish; bake at 350 degrees for 30-35 minutes or until surface springs back when pressed with finger. Ice cake with the following:

*Frosting*

| | |
|---|---|
| ⅓ cup soft margarine | 1½ tsp. vanilla |
| 3½ cups confectioners' sugar | 1 drop green food coloring |
| 3 tsp. milk | |

Mix all ingredients together until smooth. Ice cake. Top with toasted coconut or crushed peanuts if desired.

# LEPRECHAUN GREEN SPINACH AND CHEESE PIES

*(Lauding Irish love of fireworks)*

1 10-oz pkg. frozen chopped spinach
¼ lb. feta cheese (about ¾ cup)
½ cup chopped green onion
2 eggs lightly beaten
1 lb. unsalted butter

2 tbsp. butter (¼ stick)
2 tbsp. dried dill
¾ cup minced parsley
   salt; freshly ground pepper
1 pkg. phyllo leaves

Steam spinach just until defrosted. Drain; squeeze out all the moisture, and then place in large bowl. Heat the 2 tbsp. butter in small skillet. Add onions and sauté until transparent but not brown. Combine with spinach. Add feta, parsley, green onion, and dill; mix well. Thoroughly blend in eggs. Add salt and pepper to taste.

Melt ½ lb. butter in sauce pan (melt the remainder as needed). Lightly butter baking sheet. Work with one phyllo leaf at a time. (Cover remaining leaves completely with waxed paper, with damp towel over them to prevent drying out.) Place phyllo leaf on board and cut with very sharp knife into strips 2 to 2½" wide. Brush all strips with melted butter. Place 1 tsp. of filling at end of each strip. Fold each strip over and over to form a small triangle. Brush with butter and place on baking sheet.

Continue with remaining strips, working as fast as possible. Preheat oven to 425 degrees and bake triangles 15-20 minutes or until golden. Serve hot. May be frozen unbaked. When ready to use, place still-frozen triangles on buttered baking sheet and bake in preheated 425-degree oven for 20 minutes.

# April—("Purple Lace Flowers Shell")

## AN EASTER BREAD FEAST
*(The baking & breaking of bread)*

| | |
|---|---|
| 1 box lemon cake mix | ½ tsp. salt |
| 2 pkgs. dry yeast | 2½ cups warm water |
| 5-6 cups of flour | |

Take dry yeast, warm water, salt, and mix together (just blend). Put cake mix in another bowl, and pour warm-water mixture into bowl. Add 1 cup of flour at a time and mix (knead) until you have stiff dough. Let the dough rise in a glass or plastic bowl for 2-3 hours. Butter 3 bread pans, and put one-third of the dough into each pan. Let dough rise again until it reaches the top of each pan. Bake at 350 degrees for 40 minutes. Beat egg whites and glaze top of each bread.

When letting dough rise, cover with plastic that has been buttered; also cover with dish towels or cloth napkins.

## TRADITIONAL EASTER CREAMY NOODLE PUDDING
*(Grandma Thomas's recipe)*

| | |
|---|---|
| 4 oz. medium noodles, cooked | 1 tsp. vanilla |
| 2¾ cup warm milk | ¼ lb. butter, melted |
| 1 cup sugar | ¼ tsp. salt |
| 3 eggs | 1 pint sour cream (optional) |
| 8 oz. cream cheese or 8 oz. ricotta cheese | |

Add milk and sugar to cooked noodles, and set aside. In blender, put eggs, cream cheese or ricotta cheese, vanilla, melted butter, and salt. Blend all together and add to noodle-milk mixture. Bake in well-greased 3-quart pan at 350 degrees for 1 hour. Top with sour cream if desired.

# May—Memorial Day ("Blue Comets Shells")

## COMMEMORATION BLUEBERRY CARROT CAKE

*(You're never "blue" with "orange")*

| | |
|---|---|
| 2 cups all-purpose flour | 4 medium carrots, grated |
| 2 tsp. ground cinnamon | 1 tsp. baking powder |
| 1 tsp. salt | 1 cup sugar |
| 1½ tsp vanilla | 4 eggs |
| ½ cup light brown sugar | 2 cups fresh or frozen blueberries |
| 1 cup oil | 1 cup chopped nuts |

Prepare bunt pan. Combine flour, baking powder, baking salt, cinnamon, sugar, and brown sugar. Add oil, vanilla, and eggs. Mix until combined. Add nuts and carrots. Do not over-mix. The batter will be thick. Put into bunt pan. Bake at 350-degrees for 1 hour, or until cake pulls away from edges of the pan. Top with Cool Whip and blueberries. Refrigerate.

## A MEMORIAL DAY ROCKETing RICE PUDDING

*(Annlyn's favorite)*

| | |
|---|---|
| 4 cups 2% or whole milk | 1 egg |
| ¼ lb. butter | ½ pint heavy cream or light cream |
| ¾ cup sugar | 1 tsp. vanilla |
| Bring above to slow boil, and add: | cinnamon (for sprinkling on top |
| 1 cup cooked rice, cooled | when done) |
| Lower flame to simmer and cook | |
| 45 minutes, stirring often. | |

Beat together egg and cream and add to the cooked rice. Mix thoroughly. Put in a serving dish and let cool. Stir in the vanilla. Sprinkle with cinnamon. Refrigerate.

# MAYPOLE TORTELLINI SALAD
*(Grandfather Thomas's favorite)*

1 pkg. (9 oz.) refrigerated or dried cheese-filled tortellini

1 pkg. (9 oz.) refrigerated or dried spinach tortellini

⅔ cup nonfat Italian dressing

2 tbsp. chopped fresh basil leaves

1 tbsp. freshly grated Parmesan cheese

2 tbsp. capers and ⅛ tsp. pepper

2 medium carrots, sliced (about 1 cup)

2 green onions, chopped

Cook tortellini; drain. Rinse with cold water; drain. Place tortellini and remaining ingredients in large glass or plastic bowl; toss to coat tortellini with dressing. Cover and refrigerate about 2 hours or until chilled. Toss again before serving (makes about 6 servings).

# June—Anniversary/Wedding
# ("Diamonds in the Sky Shells")

# GEORGE & CONNIE'S ANNIVERSARY BANANA CAKE
*(Award-winning recipe)*

2 cups brown sugar

3 well beaten eggs

⅜ cup sour cream

¾ tsp. baking soda

1½ cups mashed bananas

¾ cup shortening

1½ tsp. vanilla

3 cups flour

¾ tsp. salt

1 container Cool Whip or whipping cream (If using whipping cream, whip it just before using)

additional banana, sliced, for decoration

Cream shortening and sugar. Add eggs & vanilla, and beat until fluffy. Add dry ingredients, alternating with sour cream and mashed bananas. Beat well after each addition. Bake in two greased cake pans. Place in 350-degree oven for 30 minutes. Cool and frost. Cut into layers. Top with whipping cream or Cool Whip and sliced bananas. Place second layer on top, and repeat with same ingredients. Decorate with bananas.

# A WEDDING DAY "WEDDING SOUP"

*(George Zambelli, Jr.'s favorite)*

*Soup*

- 1 quart chicken broth
- ½ cup pastina
- 1 carrot, sliced thin
- ½ lb. spinach (just leafy part, julienne cut) or
    2 cups escarole
- 2 cups water
- 1 tsp. chopped fresh parsley

*Meatball mixture*

- ½ lb. lean beef
- 2 tsp. flavored bread crumbs
- 2 tsp. chopped fresh parsley
- 1 egg
- 1 tsp. grated cheese
- 1 small onion, minced

*Eggdrops*

- 2 eggs
    grated cheese

In a soup pot, combine soup ingredients and bring to a low boil. Mix meatball ingredients in a separate bowl; make tiny meatballs, and fry until cooked; drop cooked meatballs into boiling broth mixture. In a small bowl, beat the 2 eggs. With a wooden spoon, stir soup as you slowly drop in the eggs, stirring constantly. Remove from heat. Cover and let stand for 2 minutes. Serve with grated cheese.

# AUNT CONGETTA'S WEDDING COOKIES

*("Eternal bliss")*

- 1 cup sugar
- 2½ cups flour
- 4 tsp. baking powder
- 6 eggs
- 1 cup shortening
- ½ tsp. vanilla

Blend together sugar and eggs. Add shortening, baking powder, and vanilla. Add flour and mix. Form into 1" balls and place on greased cookie sheet. Bake in 350-degree oven for 10 minutes. Cool and ice with the following:

*Frosting*

- ½ cup butter or shortening
- ½ cup powdered sugar
- 1 tsp. vanilla

Cream above ingredients. Ice cool cookies.

## CELEBRATION ROASTED PEPPER QUICHE

*(An Independence Day favorite)*

1 cup chopped red roasted peppers

1 cup chopped spinach

½ tsp. salt

⅛ tsp. pepper

4 eggs—well mixed

½ cup mushrooms

½ cup shredded mozzarella cheese

1 (9") unbaked pie shell

Pour ingredients into a 9" unbaked shell. Bake 1 hour or until center of filling is firm.

## ROCKETS' RED GLARE STRAWBERRY CAKES

*(Enjoying the Fourth with number one sweets)*

½ cup of fresh (sweetened to taste) or frozen strawberries

¼ cup margarine or shortening

¾ cup sugar

1 egg slightly beaten

½ tsp. vanilla

1 cup cake flour

1 tsp. baking powder

¼ cup milk

Drain strawberries on paper towel. Cream shortening. Add vanilla and sugar, and beat well. Combine cake flour, baking powder, and salt. Add to egg, alternating with milk. Beat thoroughly. Carefully fold in strawberries. Pour into muffin cups and bake 30 minutes. Cool. Ice with vanilla frosting.

*Frosting*

2 cups confectioners' sugar

2 tbsp. milk

½ tsp. vanilla

½ cup fresh strawberries, sliced
(Add additional milk if needed.)

Sprinkle top of icing with pink sprinkles and/or sliced fresh strawberries.

# INDEPENDENCE DAY LEMON VEAL CUTLETS

*(Danabeth's favorite)*

1½ lbs. veal, sliced thin

3-4 cups flavored bread crumbs, Italian style

2 eggs beaten with a little milk

2 tsp. garlic powder

2 chicken bouillon cubes

¼ cup boiling water

2 lemons (for juice)

2 lemons sliced thin for decoration

¾ cup dry white wine or "alcohol-free" wine

¾ tbsp. olive oil

¾ tbsp. butter or margarine

¾ tbsp. grated Romano cheese or Parmesan cheese

Slice veal into medium-thin, cutlet-sized pieces. Beat eggs (with the added small amount of milk). Dip veal into egg batter, then into bread crumbs that are seasoned with salt, pepper, and garlic powder, until veal slices are nicely coated. Gently heat olive oil and margarine. Slightly brown cutlets on both sides and remove to paper towel. Dissolve bouillon cubes in ¼ cup boiling water, and pour over cutlets in a casserole dish. Bake at 325 degrees, covered with aluminum foil, for 20 minutes. Add wine and bake uncovered for 15 minutes. Sprinkle with Romano cheese before serving. Arrange lemon slices atop cutlets.

# August ("Majestic Transformation Shells")

## IMPERIAL CHEESECAKE PIE

*(A royal dish for royal fireworks watchers)*

1 (8-oz.) package cream cheese, softened

1 egg

⅓ cup sugar

½ tsp. vanilla

1 (9") unbaked, deep-dish pie shell

1 cup pecan halves

*Topping mixture*

2 eggs, slightly beaten

¼ cup sugar

⅔ cup dark corn syrup

¼ tsp. vanilla

Preheat oven to 375 degrees. In small bowl, combine cream cheese, egg, sugar, and vanilla. Beat until light and fluffy. Spread over bottom of pie shell. Arrange pecans over cream cheese mixture. Combine topping mixture (2 eggs, sugar, corn syrup, and vanilla) and carefully pour over pecans. Bake 40-45 minutes

# GALA ITALIAN SAUSAGE PIE

*("Celebrating Tarantella-style")*

2 lbs. sweet Italian sausage or turkey
   sausage

3 eggs

3 cups ricotta cheese

4 hard-cooked eggs (shelled, thinly sliced)

1 lb. grated mozzarella cheese

½ cup fresh parsley
   dash black pepper

1 (9") unbaked pie shell

Simmer sausage in large frying pan with enough water to just cover the bottom of the pan, until sausage is brown and water is gone. When cool, slice at an angle, about ¼" thick. Set aside. Combine next 6 ingredients and sausage, and mix well. Pour into unbaked pie shell. Bake at 350 degrees for 35 to 40 minutes. Serve warm or cold.

## September—Labor Day ("Burst of Wheat Shells")

## HARVEST BAKED SHORT RIBS and BEANS

*(A meal as warm as fireworks for the oncoming winter)*

1 large can baked ham

2 lbs. beef short ribs

3 tbsp. molasses

3 tbsp. brown sugar

1 tsp. yellow mustard

1 tsp. pepper

⅓ cup hot water

½ cup catsup

1 onion, diced

Mix all ingredients together and bake uncovered at 300 degrees for 4 to 5 hours.

# BOBBING APPLE WALNUT COBBLER
*(Grandma Thomas's oldest recipe)*

4 cups tart apples, pared, sliced thin

½ cup sugar

½ cup cinnamon

1 egg, beaten

½ cup evaporated milk

⅓ cup margarine or butter

1 cup sugar

1 cup enriched flour, sifted

1 tsp. baking powder

¼ tsp. salt

¾ cup walnuts, chopped

Place apples in greased round baking dish. Sprinkle with the ½ cup sugar and the cinnamon. In separate bowl, combine egg, milk, and margarine or butter. Sift together the one cup sugar, flour, baking powder and salt, and add to the milk mixture. Mix until smooth. Pour over apples, and sprinkle with nuts. Bake at 325 degrees for 45-50 minutes or until brown. Serve with ice cream.

# *October—Halloween*
## *("Shimmering Specter Shells")*

# PHANTASMIC ORANGE MANDARIN CAKE
*(Lucille Jute's favorite)*

*Cake*

1 box yellow cake mix

4 eggs

¾ cup oil

1 20-oz. can crushed pineapple with juice

1 large box instant vanilla pudding

*Topping*

1 12-oz. Cool Whip pkg.

1 11-oz. can mandarin oranges, drained

Mix together all cake ingredients. Bake in oblong pan at 350 degrees for 1 hour. Cool.

Frost cake with Cool Whip, and top with mandarin oranges. For Halloween colors, add any black trimmings (candy, licorice, etc.). Refrigerate.

# DONNALOU'S COLUMBUS DAY CHICKEN CACCIATORE

*(Better than the Niña, Pinta, and Santa Maria)*

4 boneless, skinless chicken breast halves
(about 1 lb.)

2 tbsp. olive or vegetable oil

2 cloves of garlic, finely chopped

2 tbsp. of finely chopped onion

1 cup sliced fresh mushrooms

1 medium green bell pepper
(about 1 cup, diced)

1 teaspoon red or white wine vinegar

1 large can spaghetti sauce

½ cup dry white wine or chicken broth

Between sheets of plastic wrap or wax paper, flatten each chicken breast to ¼-inch thickness. Heat oil in 10-inch skillet over medium-high heat. Cook garlic, onion, mushrooms, and bell pepper in oil for 5 minutes, stirring occasionally. Add chicken to skillet. Cook about 8 minutes, turning once, until brown. Add wine and vinegar. Cook 3 minutes. Stir in spaghetti sauce.

# *November—Thanksgiving*
# *("Glittering Gold Chrysanthemum Shells")*

## PILGRIMS' PUMPKIN PIE

*(Filling stomachs and lighting heavens)*

*Filling*

1 16 oz. can pumpkin

¾ cup brown sugar firmly packed

1 tbsp. pumpkin pie spice

½ tsp. salt

2 eggs

1 cup evaporated milk

½ cup milk

*Pie shell*

1 (9") unbaked pastry shell

*Topping*

1 12-oz Cool Whip pkg. or 1 cup whipping
cream, whipped

Combine all filling ingredients and pour into unbaked pastry shell. Bake at 425 degrees for 50 minutes. Top with whipped cream or Cool Whip.

# THANKFUL TURKEY BOMBAY

*("Gobbling" up the skies in appreciation)*

2 cups diced turkey

1 tbsp. olive oil or vegetable oil

1 tbsp. minced green pepper

2 tbsp. minced onions

½ cup chopped apple (optional)

1 cup raw rice

2 cups chicken broth

½ cup tomato juice

1 tsp. salt

⅓ tsp. pepper

2 beaten egg yolks

2 tbsp. Parmesan cheese

Slightly heat oil, pepper, and onions. Add apple (if used), rice, chicken broth, tomato juice, salt, and pepper. Add turkey and simmer until rice is cooked. If necessary, add more tomato juice. Remove from fire and add egg yolks and cheese, stirring vigorously so mixture does not curdle. Put in casserole dish and bake 25 minutes in 350-degree oven.

# MERRY HOLIDAY PIZZELLES

*(Marcy's favorite)*

2 cups all-purpose flour

1 cup sugar

¾ cup (1½ sticks) margarine or butter, melted and cooled

1 tbsp. anise extract or vanilla

2 tsp. baking powder

4 eggs, slightly beaten

Lightly grease pizzelle iron. Heat iron as directed by manufacturer. Mix all ingredients. Drop 1 tablespoon batter onto each design of heated pizzelle iron and close iron. Bake about 30 seconds, or until golden brown. Carefully remove pizzelle from iron, and cool. Repeat with remaining batter. Makes about 3½ dozen cookies.

# December—Christmas
## ("Brilliant Red and Gold Chrysanthemum Shells")

## CHRISTMAS HOLIDAY RED VELVET CAKE
*(A fiery red festivity)*

½ cup butter

2 cups sugar

2½ cups flour

¼ tsp. salt

1 cup sour milk or buttermilk

1 tsp. vanilla

½ cup shortening

4 eggs

1 tsp. baking powder

4 tbsp. cocoa

1 tbsp. red food coloring

Preheat oven to 350 degrees. Grease and flour three 9" cake pans. Cream butter, shortening, and sugar. Add eggs. Combine flour, soda, salt, and cocoa. Add gradually to creamed mixture, alternating with milk. Add vanilla and food coloring. Blend well. Pour into pans and bake 25 to 30 minutes. Cool and frost with the following recipe:

*Frosting*

1 16-oz. box confectioners' sugar

1 tsp. vanilla

4 tbsp. milk

1 cup margarine

  red food coloring

½ cup shredded coconut

Blend sugar, margarine, vanilla, and milk or buttermilk, until smooth and fluffy. Additional milk or buttermilk may be needed to achieve fluffy consistency. Frost layers and assemble. Tint coconut with red food coloring and sprinkle over top. (Sides of cakes don't have to be frosted.)

# Special Recipes for Any Occasion

## NEW MILLENNIUM MEATBALLS
*(Grandchildren's favorite)*

1  pound ground beef
½  cup dry bread crumbs
½  tsp. salt
½  tsp. pepper

½  small onion, chopped (about ¼ cup)
1  egg
¼  cup milk
⅛  tsp. garlic

Heat oven to 400 degrees. Mix all ingredients, and shape into twenty 1½" meatballs. Place in ungreased rectangular pan, 13 x 9 x 2 inches. Bake uncovered 20-25 minutes, or until no longer pink in center. Drain.

*To Panfry:* Cook meatballs in oil-coated 10-inch skillet, over medium heat, about 20 minutes, turning occasionally, until no longer pink in center. Drain. Serve along with your favorite tomato sauce or pasta (see Italian Sauce recipe on page 137).

## PASTA E FAGIOLI
*(Grandma Zambelli's favorite)*

2  garlic cloves, minced
2  tbsp. olive oil
1  16-oz. can cannellini beans
½  lb. ditalini or elbow macaroni
1  tsp. salt

1  8-oz. can tomato sauce
1  cup water
2  tbsp. fresh parsley, chopped
¼  cup grated cheese

In a sauce pan, fry the garlic gently in the oil until golden brown. Add tomato sauce and water and let cook 10 minutes. Add beans and salt; stir gently, continuing to cook on simmer. In a separate pot, boil ditalini or elbow macaroni *al dente*, and drain. Add to bean mixture. Stir gently. If too thick, add more water. Stir in parsley and grated cheese. Serve immediately or pasta will absorb all the liquid.

# Epilogue

## THE LAST WORD ON THE LAST NAME IN FIREWORKS

George Zambelli, Sr., sits at his desk, scouring papers. Behind him stands his wife Connie, looking more like a woman in her fifties than one in her early seventies. She's there to give her input, support her husband, and check on the staff, flashing a smile and singing her soft tones. In and out of George's office rush his team, including his son-in-law, daughter, secretaries, assistants, and plant personnel. If the rest of his crew isn't physically at headquarters, then they're there through phone calls, fax, and e-mail.

Now, after nearly 113 years of pyrotechnics artistry, Zambelli Fireworks Internationale is stronger than ever. Its staff runs a company that is the first, the biggest and the best in the industry. Yet, none of these people are arrogant or conceited; instead, they're overly modest, forever looking for ways to better serve their clients, give something of themselves, and become even more adroit at what they do.

Having worked with them since 1975, including the two years in creating this book, I have a deep appreciation for who and what they are, and for their time and energies in helping me accomplish this project. I would say to you readers that if this book has taught you anything about how to become successful in a country that promotes hard work as a stepping stone, or how to remain modest and charitable in the face of fame and wild success, or how to love others—starting first with family and then reaching beyond—then this book has achieved its goal.

I hope some day you're as lucky as I in finding people like the Zambelli family who will touch their hearts to yours and give you a whole new perspective on life.

— *Gianni (Nan) DeVincent Hayes, Ph.D.*
*Salisbury, MD*

*Christmas 2002, George and Connie enjoy all their beloved grandchildren gathered around them. Back row: Summer (26), Chad, George III (20), Jared (15), Jessica (23), Alison (27), Amberlee (22). Front row: Michael Jr. (14), Connie, George Sr., Aubriana (10), Constance (10). Front center: Alandra (5).*

# Appendices

## I. Zambelli Fireworks Internationale, Inc., Statistics

**Company Name:** Zambelli Fireworks Internationale, Inc.

**Location:** International headquarters: Z Penn Center: New Castle, Pennsylvania, 40 miles NW of Pittsburgh

**Founded:** 1893; Antonio Zambelli brought his pyrotechnics vision to America from his homeland of Caserta, Italy

**Rank:** America's largest exhibitor of fireworks

**Size:** Three regional offices; company reps and consultants stationed around the world; more than 50 year-round employees, with several hundred during the Fourth of July season; employs staff in departments such as Finance, Aerial Manufacturing, Accounting, Low-Level Manufacturing, Marketing, Special Effects, Manufacturing, Design, Computer/Electronics, Inventory, Choreography, Purchasing, Shipping, Program Design, Sales, PR & Customer Relations

**Function:** Displays fireworks products for indoor and outdoor use, including laser shows, cannon explosions, outdoor lighting, choreographing, and other unique and stunning effects

**Officers:** George Zambelli, Sr., President and CEO
   Connie Zambelli, Senior Vice President
   Marcy Zambelli, Vice President of Marketing
   George Zambelli, Jr., M.D., Chairman of the Board
   Annlyn Zambelli, Assistant to the President
   Danabeth Zambelli, Vice President of Sales
   Donnalou Zambelli, D.D.S., Administrative
      Consultant and Board of Directors

**Corporate Headquarters:**
Z Penn Center
P.O. Box 1463 or 20 South Mercer Street
New Castle, PA 16103
Phone: 724/658-6611; 800/245-0397
Fax: 724/658-8318
E-mail: zambelli@zambellifireworks.com

**Home Page:** www.zambellifireworks.com

### REGIONAL OFFICES:
**Southern Region:**
299 NW 52nd Terrace, Suite 118
Boca Raton, FL 33487
Phone: 561/395-0955; 800/860-0955
Fax: 561/395-1799
E-mail: zifboca@yahoo.com

**Western Region:**
P.O. Box 987
Shafter, CA 93263
Phone: 805/746-2842
Fax: 805/746-2844
E-mail: boom@lightspeed.net

Zambelli Laser Eye Institute
George Zambelli, Jr., M.D., Medical Director
380 Adams Street
Rochester, PA 15074
Phone: 800/44-LASER; 724/728-5000
Fax: 724/728-4479
E-mail: drz@zambellilasik.com

**Markets:** Company performs domestically and world-wide: United States, Europe, Asia, Africa, Australia, the Americas

**Total number of annual displays:** more than 3,500

**Approximate number of displays during week of Fourth of July:** more than 1,800

**Number of shells fired:** Over 2.5 million during Independence Day week alone

# II. Pre-eminent Zambelli Pyrotechnics Facts and Figures

*Below is a listing of some outstanding facts and figures from unique fireworks shows:*

**Greatest barge usage for a single display:** Fireworks shot from 30 barges

**Most hours to choreograph:** 720

**Greatest poundage in mortars for a single display:** 777,000 pounds mortar tubes to house explosives

**Special effects:** 11,000 waterfall effects from two bridges; waterfalls 6 to 8 times longer than the length of Niagara Falls, measuring more than 6,000 feet

**Most musical production time:** 240 hours to produce musical score

**Largest number of speakers:** 400 high-efficiency speakers stretching 1.5 miles

**Dual-country display:** Only show hosting two countries simultaneously (one in Detroit, USA; the other in Windsor, Canada), featuring the 24-inch Mother Earth "Friendship Shell"

**Longest assembly time:** Nearly two weeks to set up and assemble display, at 3360 man-hours for a 30-minute show

**Largest low-level pyrotechnics display:** Spanning nearly 1.5 miles in length

**Greatest breaking diameter:** The 24-inch Mother Earth Friendship Shell, launched to a height of 1,750 feet, with breaking diameter of 2,000 feet, weighing 180 to 200 pounds, launched from a 14-foot-long mortar 2 feet in diameter; displays in a quarter-mile radius; takes 30 seconds from launch to burnout, with a 16-second lift time and a 14-plus-second burn time

**Most popular shells:** Chrysanthemum and peonies

**Longest show:** 3 hours to fire: "Zambelli Space Wars"

**Most difficult color:** Blue is most difficult color to create

**Newest color:** Purple

**Largest set piece:** Zambelli's "Great Seal," covering 3,200 square feet, lighted by 5,200 colored lances

**Presidential shows:** Displayed for every president since and including Kennedy: 8 presidents spanning nearly 45 years

**Greatest number shells in a single display:** More than 33,000

**Greatest sand use in a single display:** 1,000,000-plus pounds

**Largest amount of wire in a single display:** 500 miles of electrical wire

**Most trucks used in a single display:** 8 tractor-trailers, along with eight 24-foot box trucks

**Most manpower in single display:** 30 pyrotechnicians with 500 years' combined experience

**Unique fireworks uses:** Funerals, weddings, divorces, lottery winnings, christenings, bar mitzvahs

**Most unusual request:** Several clients wanting their ashes placed in aerial shells and fired over their favorite locations

**Fireworks shot from highest building:** U.S. Steel Building (64 floors high; 841 feet to heliport which served as the "firing station")

**Highest land site:** Elevation 8,000 feet (Squaw Valley)

**Most challenging setup:** All equipment, explosives, and pyrotechnicians had to be transported to firing site (Mount Rushmore) by helicopter

**Greatest number of firing locations in one city:** 17 locations simultaneously in one of America's biggest cities, for a New Year's Eve celebration

**Most unusual display of a single set piece:** A set piece was hung from a helicopter and flown 700 to 1,000 feet in the air

# III. Sampling of Zambelli's Top Shows

- "Thunder Over Louisville"
- "Statue of Liberty Centennial Fireworks Spectacular"
- "Marshal Field's–Target Freedom Festival Fireworks"
- Chesapeake Jubilee
- Pittsburgh Three Rivers Regatta
- Target Aquatennial Fireworks
- "Zambelli Space Wars" Show (requires 3 hours to fire)
- Trump Plaza Fourth of July
- "National Victory Celebration":
  Desert Storm Troop Return, Washington, D.C.
- Presidential inaugurations/celebrations
  (every president, Kennedy through George W. Bush)
- Papal visits
- Canadian National Exhibition
- World's Fairs
- Super Bowls
- College Bowls (Gator, Fiesta, Orange, Sugar, Rose, Liberty)
- Bob Hope's "Honor America Day"
- QE II's Return to Great Britain post-Falklands War
- Elvis Presley Memorial Stamp unveiling
- National Boy Scout Jamborees
- Republican and Democratic National Conventions
- White House concerts
- World Space Congress
- Guam's New Year's Eve celebration
- Virgin Islands Carnival, St. Thomas
- World University Games closing ceremonies
- The Great Seal
- Opening of the Ford Library
- Opening of the Carter Center
- Opening of the Bush Library
- Iranian Hostage Welcome Home
  (at the Washington Monument)
- Implosion of Aladdin Hotel
- Kuwait's Independence Day
- World Series
- All-Star Game
- Wedding of Prince Charles and Lady Diana
- Major- and minor-league baseball teams
- NFL football teams
- NBA basketball teams
- NHL hockey teams
- "First Night" (New Year's Eve) celebrations
- "Saudi Arabia Yesterday & Today"
- Disney movie premiers
- "Mount Rushmore Independence Day Celebration"
- Las Vegas Millennium
- Other millennium shows
- White House state dinner: George W. Bush & President Vicente Fox of Mexico
- St. Louis Fair . . . Arch Grounds
  (St. Louis Arch is one of our national monuments)

And many, many others.

# IV. Awards for George Zambelli, Sr.

**Honorary Citizen of Louisville, Kentucky**
"Thunder Over Louisville 2003"

**Silver Buffalo Award**
Boy Scouts of America

**"Man of the Year" Homage**
Boys Towns of Italy

**George Zambelli Day**
Pittsburgh, PA

**Hall of Fame**
International Festivals and Events Association/
Miller Brewing Company

**Business Man of the Year**
Society of America Italian Heritage

**Distinguished Citizen**
Neshannock Township, New Castle, PA

**Outstanding Citizen of New Castle, PA**
Veterans of Foreign Wars

**"Dedication to Excellence
and Immeasurable Contributions"**
International Festivals Association

**Distinguished Alumni Award**
Century Club of Duquesne University

**"Award of Appreciation"**
Spartanburg, South Carolina

**Congressional Honor**
United States of America

**Co-Chairman**
National Boy Scouts of America

**Industrialist of the Year**
*Italian Tribune News*

**Honorary Rotarian**

**Dedicated Member of the Little League
Baseball Association**

**"We Love Erie Days" Award**
Erie, PA

**Award of Acclaim**
Pro Football Hall of Fame
Canton, Ohio

**Beta Gamma Sigma Chapter Award**
Duquesne University
Pittsburgh, PA

**Award of Distinction**
Pittsburgh Three Rivers Regatta
DiCesare Engler Production, Inc.

**Honoree of Muscular Dystrophy**
New Castle, PA

**Honorary Generale**
Italian American Collection
Historical Society of Western Pennsylvania

*"Man of the Year—National Italian American Sports Hall of Fame—Pittsburgh Chapter." George pictured with his sister, Connie, who was always by his side and there for him when he needed a hand.*

*Late 90s. George is honored with his wife, Connie. Over the years, many organizations have honored his success, his family, and his contributions to society.*

*1999 Western Pennsylvania Family Business of the Year award from the University of Pittsburgh. Back row, left to right: Summer Joy, Oscar Fumagali and Marcy, holding Alandra, Danabeth, Melanie, and George Jr. Front row, left to right: Amberlee, Connie, Aubriana, George Sr., and Alison.*

*King George and Queen Connie reign over the parade at the 2000 International Festivals and Events Association Foundation Party at Kern Studios, New Orleans, Louisiana.*

*Caesars Indiana honors George and Connie at a party kicking off the 2001 Kentucky Derby Festival and Thunder Over Louisville.*

# V. Zambelli Internationale Specialty Shells

*Listed Are a Few of the Most Popular*

**Chrysanthemums:** These colorful shells unfold in gigantic circumferential floral patterns with various colors radiating from the central core. They vary in color combinations and sectional array, and often transform from one color to another.

**Fish or Serpents:** These shells are Zambelli's famous shapes that swim through the sky, looking like miniature pinwheels spinning in the sky.

**Kamuros:** A most enchanting and stunningly exquisite fanfare of shells, presenting a brocade crown in a manner unequaled anywhere, with a breathtaking, vibrant array. These shells produce a glittering golden rain that begins high in the sky, and then drops almost to ground level. When these shells are used with dramatic and impassioned music, the results are truly spectacular.

**Magnesium rainbow comets:** Brilliant rainbow-colored comets paint the sky through the use of angled positions and Zambelli's top-of-the-line electrical shells. Lighting the sky in reds, oranges, yellows, greens, blues, purples, golds, and silvers, this kaleidoscopic effect, with magnesium comet tails, electrifies the night.

**Palm tree:** This shell leaves a feathery trunk as it climbs the sky until it reaches its trajectory, and a number of large gold or silver flitter stars are released to give the appearance of palm tree branches with green tips.

**Spiderwebs in gold:** This scene is composed of Zambelli's own spiderweb shells, which weave their way across the skyline, growing in size until the last web fades.

**Strobing sensations:** These shells are brilliant in their illumination. When fired in multiples, they create a sky full of red, green, violet, and white strobing light, especially when reflected off water.

**Pastel shells:** Brand-new to the fireworks industry, these shells delight all with their unique pastel pinks, greens, and blues painted against a black sky.

**Peonies:** A multitude of colorful stars fall like the petals of a peony flower into loose patterns of brilliant drooping trails.

**Pattern shells:** These crowd-pleasing fireworks bring out the oohs and aahs as they erupt into five-pointed stars, full circles, finely formed hearts, eloquently tied ribbons, and beaming smiley faces.

**Zambelli crossette:** Originating from one initial break that spits out aerial comets, this shell expels a number of stars into the sky. At their complete extension, they split once again to produce the "splitting comet" visual effect. This image can be made of various compositions, including flitters, spiderwebs, or pimpinella composites.

**Zambelli fusilating shell:** This shell produces a machine-gun sound effect in the sky. White-colored flashes produce 28 repeated noise effects for each case, and several cases can be contained within each fusilating shell.

**Zambelli multibreak shell:** This custom handcrafted shell from experienced Zambelli artisans consists of multitudinal combinations of pyrotechnic colors, sounds, and effects that, when fired into the air, break consecutively to display in a designated, sequential fashion, with one striking arrangement after another forming in a seemingly endless stream.

**Zambelli pupidelle:** Each break of this shell releases 12 minishells, displayed in a circular and uniform array. The 12 shells in the circumference break again and again, creating a cascade effect, followed by a grand resounding report.

**Zambelli pimpinella:** The intense burst of this shell expels tails outward in a radial fashion, producing heavy gold streamers known for their long duration and brilliance.

**Zambelli shell of shells:** This large, "magnificent shell of shells" contains several compartments that, when fired, burst into numerous patterns that break in rapid and random sequence.

**Zambelli margarete:** Similar to the functional sequence of the pupidelle, the minishells of the margarete are unique because of their extraordinary and glorious silver-colored, crackling effects.

**Zambelli gold or silver flitters:** Each metallic-powder star that expands from the break of this shell produces a trail of dense flitters, appearing almost featherlike as it falls from the skyline.

**Zambelli's famous specialty grand finale:** This electrifying and intense fireworks conclusion is unsurpassed in the industry. The phenomenal, mind-boggling audiovisual presentation of multilayered pigment combinations, geometric patterns, stunning radiance, and ear-piercing salutes is fired in a rapid, powerful frenzy that leaves spectators breathless.

# VI. In Tribute

Having met people from around the globe, the Zambellis have stamped their name on the tongues and in the hearts of many noted people. Here is a sampling of what others say to, and about, them:

*"Having been in the baseball business for quite a while, I have had an opportunity to travel and see many fireworks shows throughout the country. There is no show that comes close to the one that the Zambelli family puts on at PNC Park. Their level of expertise and creativity is a notch above everyone else in the industry. When they put on a show in our ballpark, it is guaranteed to increase attendance because everyone knows that they are in for a special treat."*

*"Just as dedicated as the Zambelli family is to fireworks, they are very involved with philanthropic endeavors throughout our region. George and Connie Zambelli have always been there to lend a hand whenever they could. We are very fortunate to have them in our community."*

— Kevin McClatchy
CEO & Managing General Partner
Pittsburgh Pirates

*"George Zambelli ignites the world with his wit, charm and expertise. The world is a brighter place with the Zambellis in it."*

— Tom Faulk,
Schwan Food Company

*"The Zambelli family is undeniably the first family of fireworks! George and Connie Zambelli have created an American institution in Zambelli Fireworks Internationale. With hundreds of millions having been 'wowed' by their spectacular pyrotechnic displays over the years, George and Connie's personal commitment to excellence and attention to detail has been passed on to the rest of the family, and ensures the Zambelli legacy will continue for generations to come!"*

— Darrel R. Stefany
President
EventMakers Corporation

*"Working with the Zambelli family has been a joy. As we at Mount Rushmore National Memorial were trying to launch a celebration of the country's Founding Fathers, it was natural to turn to the Father of Fireworks, George Zambelli. George made sure that the program at Mount Rushmore was fit for presidents. I can't thank him enough for the personal attention that made all the difference, and made our mountain come alive with celebration."*

— Diana Saathoff
Executive Director
Mount Rushmore National Memorial Society

*"Tireless work, commitment to excellence, devotion to God, family, and hospitality—these are hallmarks that characterize George and Connie Zambelli. George's intense and enthusiastic drive to exceed customers' expectations and Connie's unwavering support have complemented each other to produce the premier family business, Zambelli Fireworks Internationale, making them and their family truly the world's 'first family' of fireworks. They serve as examples for all of us."*

— Franklin and Lucille Shearer
Hershey Park
Hershey, PA

*"... another outstanding fireworks display."*

— Dennis P. Saunier
Executive Director
Pro Football Hall of Fame Festival

*"You're the talk of the town. Everyone agrees that this year's Aquatennial fireworks were the best ever."*

— Stew Widdess
VP Marketing/Business
Minneapolis, MN

*"It's hard to believe that a decade has passed since our first meeting regarding 'Thunder Over Louisville.' George, there are simply no words to express our gratitude to you and Connie for what you have brought to our community over the past years. We can only imagine how many others have made similar remarks. However, what's most dear to Pam and me is the love and friendship that you and your family have given to us. It truly outshines all fireworks."*

— Wayne and Pam Hettinger
Visual Productions Inc.
Louisville, Kentucky

*"... I have had the utmost privilege to be embraced by the whole Zambelli family, starting with George and the ever-charming Connie .... The Colorado Rockies have had the greatest relationship with the Zambellis and their fireworks family. The baseball fans of the Rocky Mountain Region have had the privilege of being overwhelmed by the most spectacular fire in the sky over the years."*

— Alan D. Bossart
Director of Promotions
and Special Events
Colorado Rockies/Coors Field

*"Only one plaudit could come close to doing George Zambelli justice: He is truly 'Lord of the Sky.'"*

— Ben Harper
Advertising Manager
Kroger Company

*"George has provided ... most professional and personal services ... always ready to step up to bat with us, and making our work together a pleasure .... The Braves have entertained our fans with numerous Zambelli Fireworks shows and have capped off each home win with a brilliant Zambelli victory fireworks display."*

— Miles McRea
Senior Director
Atlanta Braves

*"To our Connie and George Zambelli, King and Queen of Fireworks: You are the greatest friends, and you have always been the leader in not only your industry but that of tourism and special events. You truly light up our lives."*

— Lee and Carolyn Crayton
Macon Georgia International
Cherry Blossom Festival

*Over the past 40 years George Zambelli, Sr. proudly gave THE BIG ONE "Zambelli Since Fireworks" pens to his valued clients around the world.*

*"In all my years viewing fireworks, I have never seen such a show displaying not only great sound but colors and coordination through music . . . received many compliments on this year's fireworks display . . . the best display that this area has viewed."*
— Robert G. "Buddy" Bagley
Fireworks Chairman
Chesapeake Jubilee

*"What a spectacular evening! The fireworks were absolutely sensational, and once again, Zambelli Internationale thrilled millions of spectators on both sides of the Detroit River at the Marshal Field's—Target Freedom Festival Fireworks."*
— Susie Gross
Executive Director
Parade Company

*". . . the magic of Zambelli has filled the sky . . . and left hundreds of thousands of attendees . . . filled with . . . awe and wonder . . . a special magic to every show . . . not found in any shell. It is found in the pride, the service, the quality, and the true friendships that cannot be imitated or copied. George and Connie [are] the foundation of that magic . . . ."*
— Steven Wood Schmader
CFE/President
International Festival
and Events Association

*"Thank you for staging Minneapolis' best-ever fireworks show. This year's Target Aquatennial Fireworks Show was spectacular, and I am very thankful for your generous support. We always enjoy working with the entire Zambelli team."*
— Lisa Dindorf
Director of Marketing
and Special Events
Minneapolis Downtown Council

*"For as long as LARC has been in business (33 years) and with 1,000 projects in our history, any production or project that has the need for fireworks, we always recommend Zambelli. George Zambelli and the entire organization have the highest degree of integrity, quality, and safety. Any productions that we do [that] include fireworks will also include the Zambelli family.*
— Michael A. Jenkins
President
Leisure and Recreation
Concepts, Inc. (LARC)

*"As a New Castle native, I have had the great pleasure and honor of knowing George and Connie nearly all of my life. Their friendship has brought me great personal joy. Their showmanship as the undisputed King and Queen of Fireworks has delivered incomparable memories to millions of people around the world for over a half-century. Most importantly, their warmth, kindness, and caring for others is an irreplaceable gift of a lifetime. Together, they hold a special place in my heart for all eternity."*
— Ida D'Errico-Hrehocik
former Executive Vice President
Pittsburgh Three Rivers Regatta

*"It is rare . . . that relationships can be forged and maintained over . . . time. . . . There isn't anyone out there like George—a consummate professional, a true impresario and a dear friend. When George Zambelli promises the moon, he delivers the sun and the stars along with it."*
— Michael Francis
Executive Vice President Marketing
Target Corporation

*"First Family of Fireworks' says it all . . . . With Zambelli Internationale, it's not just a company name but the family name. In this business, it's not about the shells or the show; it's about safety, integrity, and trust. My relationship with George over the years may not have stopped my hair loss, but it sure has allowed me to sleep the night before a show."*
— Bill Gilmore
Executive Director
Baltimore Office
of Promotion & the Arts

*"The 'Christmas Card' fireworks added so much to the festivities. Roslyn and I appreciate your generosity."*
— President Jimmy Carter

*"Nancy and I are deeply grateful for your contributions . . . ."*
— President Ronald Reagan

*" . . . magnificent and absolutely spectacular . . . display . . ."*
— Bandar bin Sultan bin Abdul
Ambassador
Royal Embassy of Saudi Arabia

*"Bravo! Bravo! Bravo! What a magnificent display! . . . the most spectacular fireworks display this city has ever seen . . . ."*
— Gary J. Walters
Chief Usher
The White House

*"The Carters recall with pleasure the magnificent shows that you hosted for the inaugural and for the opening of the Carter Center. They send their warm best wishes to you and your family."*

— Faye Dill
Personal Assistant
to President Carter
Carter Center

*"After doing business with the Zambellis for many years, this last show was the most spectacular ever."*

— Michael Gaughn
Chairman of the Board for Coast Casinos
Las Vegas, Nevada

*"Working with George Zambelli is like dealing with family. He takes a personal interest in your event, in your organization, in your employees, in your family, and in you as an individual. George's good business sense and his genuine concern for his clients [are] instilled in the entire family. In my 18 years in the special-event business, Zambelli is the only supplier whose family I have known and who took time to know me and my family. If I could trust all other aspects of my events as much as I do my fireworks presentation, managing events would be a breeze."*
— Tom Kwiatek
former Vice President of Musikfest
President and Owner of SponsorLink

*"On behalf of the Steelers organization, I want to personally extend my gratitude to Zambelli Fireworks Internationale for their involvement [in] the final game ceremonies. The fireworks were outstanding, and the finale completed the tribute to Three Rivers Stadium."*

— Arthur J. Rooney II
Vice President and General Counsel
Steelers

*"Having been responsible for orchestrating two of the nation's largest fireworks displays, I turned to the Zambellis. You can rest assured that you will have a spectacular show!"*
— Kirk Hendrix
President & CEO
500 Festival (Indianapolis)

*February 28, 1994. Great Britain's Prime Minister John Major, accompanied by President Clinton, visits Pittsburgh, where his grandfather once worked in the mills.*

# Glossary of Fireworks Terms

*(For a list of the various "Basic Types of Fireworks," see Chapter 8)*

The words used by pyrotechnicians to describe the details of their craft are nearly as colorful as the displays themselves. Here's a sampling of frequently used fireworks terms:

## GENERAL

**Aerial shell:** A cartridge or canister containing pyrotechnic compositions, a long, quick match fuse or electric match squib, and a black-powder lift charge. These shells, which detonate in the air, are securely set inside mortars. They're manufactured in cylindrical or spherical shapes and are usually 3" to 16" in diameter and weigh up to 180 pounds. When fired, the fuse and lift charge burn to discharge them from the mortars in which they're housed.

**Black match:** A type of fuse used for igniting fireworks devices; made from string saturated with black powder.

**Black powder:** A ground-up mixture of potassium nitrate, sulfur, and charcoal used as both a propellant and a bursting charge.

**Colors:** Six basic colors are used: white, yellow, red, green, blue, and orange or amber. The difficult-to-create color blue has been mastered by Zambelli Internationale.

**Comets:** A type of firework composed of a large pellet of pyrotechnic composition. When a charge of black powder is ignited, the device is either propelled from a mortar tube or discharged from an aerial canister, leaving trails (hence its name) of sparks in the air that may burst into smaller fragments.

**Electric ignition:** A process whereby one end of an electric match (squib) is attached to the fireworks device to be detonated, and the other end is hooked to an electrical firing unit or remote-control center where the operator times and controls its ignition.

**Finale:** A term for the end of a fireworks show when aerial fireworks—via chain-fusing—are rapidly and sequentially fired in a barrage or cannonade stream. Zambelli's unrivaled traditional grand finales are brilliant, colorful, and multidimensional; they conclude with forceful, resounding pyrotechnics.

**Fireworks:** Any composition or device for the purpose of producing a visible or audible effect by combustion, explosion, deflagration, or detonation.

**Flash (salute) powder:** An explosive pyrotechnic composition consisting of a heavy metal, potassium chlorate, and sulfur that makes a loud resounding report (the "boom") when ignited.

**Fuse:** A string of woven threads containing gunpowder that ignites the charges of all types of pyrotechnics materials.

**Manual ignition:** Unlike electric ignition, this is a technique whereby pyrotechnics ignite a shell's fuel source (e.g., fuse) via a handheld ignition source.

**Mortar:** Launching tube made of heavy cardboard, plastic, or metal sunk into the ground, or into a sand-filled mortar boxes, or mounted in racks.

**Mortar rack:** A strong, reinforced frame housing several mortars of the same or varying sizes, and often used for finales or barrages in electrically ignited displays.

**Parachutes:** A miniature parachute used in aerial shells to suspend various effects, including flares, colored chains, or illuminated flags.

**Quick match:** A special type of black match surrounded by a paper tube. When ignited, the sheath keeps the temperature of the fuse inside so hot that it burns extremely rapidly (approximately 60 feet per second). It is used as a long leader fuse for aerial shells, and for the simultaneous ignition of other types of pyrotechnic devices, such as the lances of a set piece.

**Smoke:** Foglike effect of various colored compositions, available in assorted types and durations.

**Special effects:** Zambelli can customize any shell with effects such as confetti cannons, streamers, flags, parachutes, and other materials.

**Squib:** Two electrical wires spun or coiled together and attached at one end; this end is covered with a mixture (composite) of potassium chlorate and sulfur, and is then covered with a resin to protect it from moisture; the other ends of the wires are individually attached to the positive and negative terminals of the electrical firing unit. When the electrical circuit is completed, the mixture (composite) detonates and lights the pyrotechnic fuse.

**Stars:** Pyrotechnics chemical pellets of varying sizes and shapes packaged in aerial shells, mines, or Roman candles. Stars burn while in the air, producing colorful patterns or streamer effects.

## OUTDOOR FIREWORKS EFFECTS

**Battle in the clouds:** A number of salutes timed to explode in rapid-fire series, sounding like a fusillade of musketry.

**Chrysanthemum:** Resembling the flower from which this firework obtained its name, the shell consists of a multitude of stars that burst simultaneously into a radial arrangement from a central core, creating a perfectly circular formation. Variations include a center or outer circumference of another color.

**Hummers:** Small tubes that spin and create a screaming or humming sound as the shells burst and gas is permitted to travel out of the tubes.

**Patterns:** Configurations of star compositions that explode to create a desired shape, such as 5-pointed stars, hearts, yellow ribbons, and smiley faces.

**Peonies:** A colorful pattern of stars that explode from a central burst and fall like the petals of a peony flower into a loose pattern of drooping trails.

**Salutes:** These are the concussive "booms" that end most shows with a loud report; there are two different types of salutes: standard and titanium.

**Set piece:** A wooden framework set on the ground and studded with lances that, when ignited, outline a portrait or picture in colored fire. Zambelli artisans can add animation to these traditionally stationary pieces.

**Strobes:** Clusters of flashing silvery lights that appear to float slowly to the ground, perceived visually as having a disco-strobe effect.

**Tourbillon:** An ignited shell that spins like a top and bounces across the skyline in a topsy-turvy dance as it rises.

**Weeping willows:** Star colors that burn an amber hue as they fall, outlining the drooping branches of the willow tree.

**Whistles:** Noisemaking tubes that dart across the sky, giving off shrieks and whistling effects as the shell bursts.

## CLOSE PROXIMITY PYROTECHNICS EFFECTS

**Airburst:** Miniature version of "Fourth of July" aerial burst, producing a brilliant drift of sparkles 3 to 30 feet in diameter; offers a visual registry of one to two seconds and a high audio registry consisting of a "pop." Available in silver or gold; one of the most popular indoor effects.

**Coliseum pot:** Brilliant flash of white light 15 to 18 feet high and 10 feet wide; gives a medium audio registry consisting of a "poof"; lasts one second.

**Concussion:** Cannonlike effect fired from a concussion mortar with a bright flash of light, accompanied by an extremely loud audio registry consisting of a "boom" and lasting one-tenth of a second.

**Fast sparkle pot:** Brilliant sparkling-silver "bush-shaped" effect 3 to 12 feet high and 5 feet wide, with low audio registry containing a "hiss" sound lasting a half-second.

**Flame projector:** Intense white, yellow, green, or red flame, 3 to 15 feet high; offers low audio registry of a "whoosh" nature, and lasting 1½ seconds.

**Fountain gerb:** Sparkling silver or gold "bush-shaped" effect, blossoming 3 to 20 feet high and 8 feet wide, with low "hiss" audio registry; of 25 to 30 second duration.

**Glitter mine:** Discharges a brilliant stream of bright gold sparkles 20 to 80 feet high, lasting 1½ seconds.

**Grid-line rocket:** Rocket effect that travels along an aircraft cable up to 80 feet; discharges a 2-foot-long brilliant red flame.

**Puff pot:** Brilliant flash of light with a ring of white smoke; has low audio registry consisting of a "poof" sound, lasting about 15 seconds.

**Slow sparkle pot:** Vertical fountain of silver cascading sparkles 3 to 15 feet high by 3 feet wide; low "swoosh" sound.

**Smoke:** Colored smoke compositions of varying types and durations.

**Spinner gerb:** Spinning discharge of silver sparkles 5 to 40 feet in diameter; visual registry of 5 to 30 seconds.

**Waterfall gerb:** Dazzling cascade of silver sparkles suspended overhead up to 40 feet wide, with a visible duration of up to 30 seconds; this effect can create a solid curtain of sparkles across the entire width of a stage or auditorium.

*The Rose Bowl, one of Zambelli's most memorable and prestigious pyro-musicals enhanced with a multitude of animated set pieces and special pyrotechnics effects.*

# Notes

1. Kuklin, Susan. *Fireworks*. New York: Hyperion, 1996.
2. St. Brock, Alan. *A History of Fireworks*. London: George G. Harrap & Co., Ltd., 1946.
3. Plimpton, George. *Fireworks*. New York: Doubleday & Co, 1984, pp. 31, 34.
4. Ibid, pp. 29–31.
5. *Seventeen* magazine, "4th of July Facts"; *The Spin*, July 1997.
6. Video. Smithsonian Institution.
7. Ibid.
8. http://cpsc.gov/cpscpub/prerel/prhtml197/97010.html "News from CPSC," Oct. 25, 1996.
9. Many of the following accounts come in part from: *Fireworks*, by Norman D. Anderson and Walter R. Brown (New York: Dodd Mead, 1983); and from *A History of Fireworks*, by Alan St. Brock (London: Harrap, 1949).
10. Plimpton, George. *Fireworks*. New York: Doubleday & Co., 1984, pp. 145–50.
11. *Fireworks in America*, "Fireworks-Related Injury Rates 1976–1995," Washington, DC: National Council on Fireworks Safety Inc., May 1966.
12. Ibid.
13. The . . . U.S. CPSC. http//www.cpsc.gov./cpscpub/pubs/july4/fireinjr.html
14. World Socialist Web site, Chris Marsden; 16 May 2000. http://www.wsws.org/articles/2000May/fire-m16.shtml
15. BBC News—Asia Pacifica. http://www.news.bbc.uk/1/world/asia-pacific/1206665.stm
16. North Kitsap Fire Rescue; December 27, 2002.
17. CNN.com; http://cnn.worldnews.printhis.clickability .com/pt/cpt?action=cpt&expire
18. Daily Southtown. Julie Watson, *Associated Press*. January 2, 2003. http://www.dailysouthtown.com/ southtown/dsnews/024nd3.htm
19. "*Fireworks in America*, "Fireworks-Related Injury Rates 1976–1995," Washington, DC: National Council on Fireworks Safety Inc., May 1966.

# Index

Page numbers in *italic* indicate photographs and illustrations.

# About the Author

Gianni DeVincent Hayes, Ph.D., has been writing professionally for more than 20 years, having earned her Ph.D. *summa cum laude* in English, creative writing, and comparative literature from the University of Maryland College Park. Both of her master's degrees were earned at Duquesne University, also with high honors, and her bachelor's degree at Gannon University, where she was honored with a *Distinguished Alumni* Award. Additionally, she attended the University of Pittsburgh for 2 years, where she earned a *Letter of Highest Commendation*, and has been in the University of Rochester's writing program for 8 summers, as well as Middlebury College's prestigious Bread Loaf Writer's Conference.

Hayes has published more than 100 articles and short stories in national magazines such as *Woman's Day, Redbook, US, People, Brides, Parade, Writer's Digest,* and many other works. In addition to her byline, she writes under various pen names, and has appeared on dozens of national radio and television shows, including *A&E Biography,* and in countrywide newspapers and magazines. Recently she completed her 50th radio/TV station interview on the subject of globalism. An internationally recognized writer, she is the recipient of many tributes, a former college professor and department chair, and author of many fiction and nonfiction books.

Gianni also writes screenplays, one of which has been optioned by a movie company. Besides her media appearances, she does book tours, seminars, signings, and readings of her work. Her columns have been syndicated nationally and internationally by Artists' Market. Her novels appear in e-book form as well, and she travels the world on cruises where she speaks about her writing and the topic of "Globalism and American Sovereignty." She is also an expert in eschatology, which combines religion, politics, philosophy, history, and Biblical prophecy. She is the honored guest at many author's receptions, has been featured in the *Contemporary Authors* encyclopedia and has been asked to donate her manuscripts to the libraries of the University of Maryland College Park for a permanent collection.

Hayes was also nominated for the Governor's Award of Writing by a state senator, a state delegate, an area council president, and several high-profile people, and was honored at her undergraduate college for Women's History Month 2003, where she gave a campus-wide presentation. She also has been unanimously voted into her high school Hall of Fame.

When not writing, Dr. Hayes enjoys university teaching, oil painting, and listening to classical music, along with spending time with her husband and daughters.